Context-Aware Mobile Computing

Affordances of Space, Social Awareness, and Social Influence

Synthesis Lectures on Human-Centered Informatics

Editor
John M. Carroll, Edward M. Frymoyer Professor of Information Sciences and Technology,
Penn State University

Context-Aware Mobile Computing: Affordances of Space, Social Awareness, and Social Influence
Geri Gay

ISBN: 978-3-031-01059-0 paperback

ISBN: 978-3-031-02187-9 ebook

DOI: 10.1007/978-3-031-02187-9

A Publication in the Springer series

SYNTHESIS LECTURES ON HUMAN-CENTERED INFORMATICS

Lecture #4

Series Editor: John M. Carroll, Pennsylvania State University

Series ISSN
ISSN 1946-7680   print
ISSN 1946-7699   electronic

Context-Aware Mobile Computing
Affordances of Space, Social Awareness, and Social Influence

Geri Gay
Cornell University

SYNTHESIS LECTURES ON HUMAN-CENTERED INFORMATICS # 4

ABSTRACT

The integration of ubiquitous mobile computing resources into physical spaces can potentially affect the development, maintenance, and transformation of communities and social interactions and relations within a particular context or location. Ubiquitous mobile computing allows users to engage in activities in diverse physical locations, to access resources specific to the location, and to communicate directly or indirectly with others. Mobile technologies can potentially enhance social interactions and users' experiences, extend both social and informational resources available in context, and greatly alter the nature and quality of our interactions. Activities using mobile devices in context generate complex systems of interactions, and the benefits of ubiquity and mobility can be easily lost if that complexity is not appreciated and understood. This monograph attempts to address issues of using and designing location-based computing systems and the use of these tools to enhance social awareness, navigate in spaces, extend interactions, and influence others.

KEYWORDS

activity theory, configuration theory, context-aware computing, HCI, location-based computing, mobile computing, place and space, social awareness, social facilitation, social influence, social navigation, social presence, motivation, ubiquitous computing

Acknowledgments

This monograph represents the combined effort of many researchers and designers from the HCI Laboratory at Cornell University from 1995 to the present. In addition, a number of agencies, foundations, and individuals funded the interdisciplinary research, evaluation, and design studies described in this volume, including IBM, IBM-Japan, Intel, the National Institutes of Health, the National Science Foundation, the Robert Wood Johnson Foundation, and the Mellon Foundation. In particular, I would like to acknowledge the following individuals for their contributions: Phil Adams, Alex Ainslie, Brian Alson, Jon Baxter, Kirsten Boehner, Jenna Burrell, Sahara Byrne, Dan Cosley, Nicholas Farina, Amy Gonzales, Jenna Holloway, Kiyo Kubo, J. P. Pollak, Phoebe Sengers, Jenn Thom-Santelli, and Emily Wagner.

I also want to thank Patrick Castrenze and Deborah Trumbull for reviewing the manuscript and making many helpful suggestions for improvement.

Contents

CHAPTER 1

Introduction

We have moved far beyond the days when computers were huge pieces of equipment stored in warehouse-sized spaces and only used by a handful of companies and university research organizations. Today, computing power is found in a range of small, everyday devices and appliances, and the use of these technologies is much more pervasive. These ubiquitous computing devices can be used to strengthen communication and awareness between users as well as with the physical environments in which these devices are used (Low and Altman, 1992; Goffman, 1971; Lyman and Scott, 1967). Context-aware computing is subsumed within the category of ubiquitous computing, and includes both the familiar and relatively simplistic, such as call forwarding on a cell phone when someone is unavailable; location aware applications using global positioning technology (Global Positioning System, Geographic Information System) that can be used to determine the position of the user in order to disseminate or receive information that may or may not be of interest to the user; the more futuristic world of intelligent sensors/appliances (e.g., smart home design, location-based shopping, smart phones that detect activities and availability).

When designing context-aware tools, especially for mobile computing technologies, it is crucial to recognize the reciprocal relationship between context and activities. The ability to detect context is especially relevant to mobile and ubiquitous systems that may be used in a variety of locations, by different users, and for different purposes. In this monograph, user behavior is presented as an element of context: where and when people congregate, how many people are present, and how long are all indications of activity occurring in a location. Certain aspects of context such as time, location, and density are easily be detected by a mobile device, but others, such as what people are doing in a particular location, is much more difficult to determine. People, on the other hand, are quite good at detecting, interpreting, and understanding activity. In our research, we have been interested in building and testing systems that allow users to play a role in interpreting context rather assigning that task to the mobile devices. By forging a partnership between the context-detecting device and the context-detecting user, a more useful and powerful system will result. Understanding how these levels of context influence and impact computing is critical for the design of useful, effective context-aware technologies.

Developing relevant aware applications then requires that we understand context as an interactive system with overlapping components. Thus, it must include not only the external physical context, but also the context the individual brings to the situation, the context of the tool/device, the information context, and finally the context created by the activity itself. Defining these levels, the levels within each level, and how they overlap with one another provides us with an understanding of how well the tools' intended purpose get translated to the individual vis-a-vis how the individual interprets these layers of context (Gay and Hembrooke, 2004).

This monograph uses *activity theory* (Engestrom et al., 1999) as an organizational framework to explicate the various elements that comprise context-aware computing (Figure 1.1). Each section emphasizes a different element of activity theory but recognizes that it is impossible to describe the impact of any one element in the system without including the other elements in the analysis. Furthermore, context is dynamic because the sequences of actions carried out in a given context are fluid and responsive to changes in the social and physical setting. Activity theory is consistent with Suchman's (1987) theory of situated action, which suggests that cognition and planned activities are inexplicably connected, and that both are the by-product of the social and physical interactions the individual is involved with in their environment.

Fundamental to activity theory, as well as other sociocultural approaches, is that humans develop and learn when, in collaboration with others, they act on their immediate surroundings (Nardi, 1996; Engestrom et al., 1999). Gidden's (1979) theory of structuration states that on one hand human action is restricted by properties of social and cultural systems, whereas on the other hand these properties are themselves the product of human action.

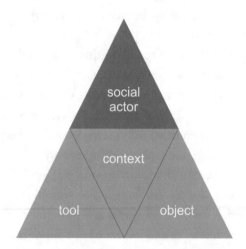

FIGURE 1.1: In activity theory, an activity consists of the actor (an individual or group), the object or motive, the tool, and the context (Engestrom et al., 1999).

Activity theory posits that context as meaningful to human actors emerges as a result of the activities that occur in a given setting. As the setting and the artifacts within the setting encourage different activities, these activities change, thus changing the context in turn (Engestrom et al., 1999; Leont'ev, 1981; Nardi, 1996). Within an activity-centered framework, activity provides the context within which an individual or group of individuals interact in the pursuit of some object or goal. Rules and roles operating in the context affect a user's behavior. Actions are assumed to be intentional, and carried out through various routinized operations using mediating devices or artifacts that, in turn, are dynamically shaped by social and physical environments (Engestrom et al., 1999; Nardi, 1996; Gay and Hembrooke, 2004).

Central to activity theory is the connection between participation, action, and understanding of the context, including physical context, and/or responding to the affordances of a particular tool. In activity theory, the focus is on the individual, and context is not a defined set of properties, but an emergent, fluid aspect unleashed by the activities imposed upon it. Thus, rather than a physical entity, context is "an operational term: something is 'in context' because of the way it is used for interpretation, not due to its inherent properties" (Winograd, 2001, p. 405).

I am taking an integrative approach in this monograph and describing the interacting components of context-aware computing. Each chapter will emphasize one aspect in the Activity Theory framework (context, social aspects, and tools). Each chapter begins with an overview of relevant theories and issues, and ends with a case study. In the next chapter, "Space, Place, and Context," the notions of context, space, place, and a sense of place are described and applied to how they can influence users' appropriation of technology for new activities. In the third chapter, "Creating a Sense of Presence and Awareness with Mobile Tools," I report on the work that my colleagues and I have done to examine theories of social awareness. By designing mobile systems to allow users to leave annotations or tag spaces, a sense of community or attachment to a particular space evolved as people developed a richer awareness of those around them, as well as developed a better understanding of the spaces and environment around them. In the fourth chapter, "Mobile Computing: A Tool for Social Influence to Change Behavior," I describe work showing how mobile devices can be used to influence attitudes and behavior, and how messages can be tailored to be presented at the right time in the right place. Although I deal with ethical and privacy issues throughout the monograph, the final chapter, "Ethical Issues and Final Thoughts," ends with a summary of the potential and the issues that surround the use of mobile tools and technologies.

· · · ·

CHAPTER 2

Space, Place, and Context

2.1 SPACE, PLACE, AND CONTEXT

2.1.1 Space

According to Cresswell (2004, p. 10), "Space has been seen in distinction to place as a realm without meaning—as a 'fact of life,' which, like time, produces the basic coordinates for human life." Spaces are often regarded as having areas, volumes, or coordinates on a map, and can be understood as abstract or general representations of physical settings and the activities or associations that evolve there (Hubbard et al., 2004; Tuan, 1977). Space has also been called "the structure of the world; it is the three-dimensional environment, in which objects and events occur, and in which they have relative position and direction" (Harrison and Dourish, 1996, p. 2). Place as a concept, on the other hand, explicitly encompasses the meanings given to places by individuals (Dourish, 2006).

2.1.2 Place

Place has been defined in human–computer interaction (HCI) as "a space with something added—social meaning, convention, cultural understandings about role, function and nature...." (Harrison and Dourish, 1996, p. 3). However, in the fields of geography and critical theory, for example, the distinction between space and place serves as a lens for exploring the mutually constitutive relationship of structure, both physical and cultural, and agency. Place is more encompassing than space, and emerges as the "lived experiences of people" (Hubbard et al., 2004; Tuan, 1977). Experience lies at the heart of place. However, this is not limited to person-to-person (space-based) experience. For example, it is no longer *necessary* that two people walking their respective routes to work every day share in a place-making experience when they encounter each other at an intersection. Although this experience may very well add to their sense of the space of their meeting as a place, Massey (1997) would argue that an equal sense of place can be created through online networks, for instance. Following her work, "A Global Sense of Place," places can, in fact, be a product of a larger global web of influence:

> "This time, however, imagine not just all the physical movement, nor even all the often invisible communications [of place], but also and especially all the social relations, all the links

between people. Fill it in with all those different experiences of time-space compression. For what is happening is that the geography of social relations is changing. In many cases such relations are increasingly stretched out over space. Economic, political and cultural relations, each full of power and with internal structures of domination and subordination, stretched out over the planet at every level, from the household to the local area to the international." (pp. 68–69)

In applied sciences such as forestry, urban planning, and conservation, progress is also being made toward understanding place, as contrasted to space, by valuing and measuring the lived experiences in places. These measurements attempt to quantify people's emotional investment or identity dependence. In the above-mentioned fields, these human dimensions of space have been typically overlooked, but if activities *do* occur, how they occur, what they mean, and what value is placed on these activities are all part of place formation. Because of the dependence on how a technology is appropriated for place-making, Harrison and Dourish (1996) emphasize not designing place *into* an object, but designing *for* place.

Harrison and Dourish (1996) first popularized the idea of place for HCI by contrasting the physical and generic space of a "house," to the personal space of a "home" and the memories, identity formation, and interactions that transpire there. However, this distinction between space and place has been criticized for implying an a priori nature of space—a blank canvas on which place is created, because what is registered as a space is shaped by prior knowledge and experience. Others have suggested alternate visions of space as being an emergent phenomenon as well. Brown and Perry (2002), for example, suggest that the important dichotomy is not between physical tangible constructs, such as the spatial configuration of a room, and the nonphysical overlays of meaning, value, and emotion. Instead, they argue the space-place dichotomy is more usefully understood as the ongoing dynamic between abstract representations (whether these be physical, political, cultural, and/or historical attributes) of space and lived experiences of place. In other words, the "sense of a place" (place in the abstract or space) and "place-making" are mutually constitutive (Dourish, 2006).

The current emphasis in HCI on supporting "experience," as opposed to "tasks" (McCarthy and Wright, 2003), echoes the view of places as supporting complex, affective, and meaning-making activities. Harrison and Dourish (1996) were among the first to emphasize the importance of place for technology design. Whereas many digital systems at the time used spatial metaphors to organize online information and activities, Harrison and Dourish (1996) argue that physical attributes of space are only part of behavioral framing. Whether particular activities would or could occur depends less on physical and temporal dimensions, but more on social and cultural conventions. Their principle is that "space is the opportunity, but place is the understood reality" (p. 4), and a sense of place is "a communally held sense of appropriate behaviour and a context for engaging in and interpreting action" (Harrison and Dourish, 1996, p. 70).

We have found sense of place discussions in HCI and in the broader literature a useful frame for thinking about the design of technology to enhance experiences in public places. In particular, we examined the interplay between abstract representations and actual behaviors or experiences in place. Moreover, we are afforded the opportunity to examine how context-aware technology may be designed as a stimulus for reflecting on existing behaviors in environments (ie, appropriate behaviors) and how technology simultaneously may provoke new behaviors or new conceptions of what constitutes appropriate behavior (Agre, 1997; Sengers, 2004).

In the case study, I will describe projects designed to enhance visitors' experiences in museums. This work combines attention to both real and virtual spaces. Before the case study, I review theories that help conceptualize space, place, and context relations.

2.1.3   Context

Once we attend to the features that make a space a place, we must also consider context, both the context of the person—a user—and the context of the place. Context-aware applications challenge our traditional notions of space by also looking at *place* and *context* as key components that need to be considered when designing mobile applications. By attending to all three—space, place, and context—we afford ourselves the opportunity to expand our imaginations by thinking outside of the space-based construct, to see how these features can be used to design tools for use in various physical contexts.

Context has traditionally been studied in HCI to describe a location, an identity, and the objects involved (Dey, 2001), but as research continues it is evident that scholars must expand this conception of context. Dey defines context as "any information that can be used to characterize the situation of an entity. An entity is a person, place, or object that is considered relevant to the interaction between a user and an application, including the user and the applications themselves" (p. 4). In this definition, Dey expands upon previous ideas of context by incorporating the notion of place. However, to further supplement or elaborate on this definition, context must include the external environment, the personal context that is carried by the individual, the context of the tool or device, the information context, and finally, the context created by the tool or device supported by the activity itself. And although attempts have been made to outline prescribed, generic definitions of these contextual layers (Dey et al., 2001), an effort that underscores the importance of identifying contextual features, scholars have typically only focused on the location-based and identification-based attributes of context. More importantly, they fail to recognize the dynamic nature of contextual influences and the interplay between and across the layers. Given the complexity of context and the various functions that aware technologies could conceivably manifest, Greenberg (2001) argues that simple taxonomies may be "difficult or impossible for a designer/programmer to test a priori" (p. 259).

Developing relevant aware applications requires us to redefine some of the core concepts that HCI research has been working with in recent years. We must understand context as a multidimensional construct with overlapping interpenetrating layers that interact to varying degrees. We must understand space as a fluid construct that gives us only a reference point from which to build other notions, such as place.

2.2   IMPLICATIONS FOR DESIGNING CONTEXT-AWARE COMPUTING

Context-aware applications challenge traditional conceptions of space as just a "place," as well as expand our imaginations for what activities might be designed using these computer tools in the varied physical contexts in which they may be used. Places are "spaces invested with understandings of behavioural appropriateness, cultural expectations, and so forth" (Harrison and Dourish, 1996, p. 71). People make assumptions about social processes in spaces and places. In addition, their activities are shaped by space, that is, spaces, the objects within them, and the events that transpire there all encourage and afford certain behaviors (Gibson, 1979). The design of real or virtual spaces should suggest the type of activity or interaction associated with the space. People orient to the affordances that exist in places and they tend to adapt practices from the physical world to the affordances of electronic space, at least initially. Furthermore, in developing tools, we must consider not only place but also context in which the tool is to be used, since a user will be influenced by actual space. The apparent same space may evoke different interpretations of appropriate behavior at different times, and Harrison and Dourish (1996) caution that spaces that do not clearly provide a "sense of place" may adversely affect communication and behavior. Therefore, computer applications should concentrate on supporting an appropriate sense of place.

Developing relevant aware applications requires us to redefine context. Using *activity theory* as a framework suggests that program development must attend not only space, the external physical context, but also to the context the individual brings to the situation, the context of the tool/ device, the information context, and finally the context created by the activity itself. Defining these levels and sublevels, and looking at how they overlap with one another, can provide us with an understanding of how well the tools' intended purpose is interpreted by the individual users as they negotiate these interpenetrating layers of context (Gay and Hembrooke, 2004).

Widening the lens of space beyond mere physical constructs underscores that in designing for place, we must consider abstract representations not as objective forms giving rise to place, but as being equally informed by place. In other words, space does not beget or simply provide the staging ground for place formation, but rather, both inform each other. Abstract representations of a place are culturally as well as physically influenced in the same manner that a sense of place develops from cultural appropriation of spaces (Boehner et al., 2005a). In fact, one could argue that a "sense of place" is actually an abstract representation, whereas place-making, or creating a sense of place, represents the lived experience. Therefore, although we may state our objective as designing for place, we cannot ignore the ongoing influence and impact of space as well (Boehner et al., 2005a).

2.2.1   Broadening the Notion of Context in Context-Aware Computing

Historically, research in context-aware computing has focused primarily on the problem of sensing and interpreting context (Spreitzer and Theimer, 1993), creating a clear definition of context and context awareness (Dey and Abowd, 2000), describing the design of various context-aware systems (Dey, Abowd and Salber, 2001), and the ability to attach information to a physical location as the user interacts with the device and the physical environment (Abowd et al., 1997). One of the most well-known context-aware systems is the Xerox Parctab project, which provides services such as call forwarding and interaction tracking in a corporate campus environment (Want et al., 1992). Several researchers have created location-aware tour guides that use Global Positioning System coordinates, infrared transceivers, or object detection to determine the user's location. Location-aware guides have been designed for city tours (Cheverst et al., 2000) and frequently for museums (Broadbent and Marti, 1997; Woodruff et al., 2001). A series of similar systems usually grouped under the term augmented reality rely on elaborate head-mounted and wearable displays (Feiner, 2002; Rekimoto and Nagao, 1995). A few researchers have even begun exploring the idea of incorporating content created by users into these location-aware guidance systems (Espinoza et al., 2001; Burrell et al., 2002; Pascoe, 1997).

A number of proponents of context-aware computing suggest that a system that can take into account the context of use can also cater more specifically to its users. The ability to detect context seems especially relevant to mobile and ubiquitous computing systems that may be used in a variety of different locations, by different users, and/or for different purposes. Standard computer features such as automatic tracking and detection can be augmented by additional features that can support what people do well such as annotating, commenting, and interpreting. These additional features expand our view of context to include social activities.

The next section uses theories of architecture and landscape design to examine ways to extract structure within and across different spaces and places. Identifying patterns and movement in and between these spaces is critical for understanding and designing spaces to support computing activities. Several techniques from architecture theory, specifically *configuration theory* and the *non-discursive techniques* used in the architecture field to design buildings, towns, and cities, can be used as a lens for understanding complex interactions between the physical and virtual spaces in context-aware computing design and applications.

2.3 NAVIGATING SPACE: ARCHITECTURAL THEORIES

There are a number of architectural theories that try to define the rules of space and the elements of spatial design. With the analysis of spaces and the adoption of architectural urban planning indices, designers focus on making physical environments legible to support specific social uses (Lynch, 1960; Alexander et al., 1977; Whyte, 1988; Hillier, 1996). Lynch grounds his work in how people perceive and organize spatial information as they navigate through cities. Using Boston, Los Angeles, and Jersey City as examples, Lynch found that users formed mental maps using five elements—*paths*, *edges*, *districts*, *nodes*, and *landmarks*—to help them understand the overall legibility of the city.

Hillier et al. (1984) address the question of how certain material arrangements foster certain forms of social interaction. Spatial syntax, or a quantified representation of space, offers Hillier's view of the city's structure and development based on aggregates of individuals' movements. Hillier found that the aggregate pattern of use and meaning for people could be correlated with statistical consistency in people's paths. He based his views of a city's structure and development on these averages or aggregates of an individual's movements (pp. 90–324). In other words, the number of access points to a spatial element, when combined with the nature of its relationship to other spaces, expresses and has impact on social characteristics such as a sense of community (Hillier, 1996, p. 376). Therefore, the author focuses on ways to extract structure within and across different spaces and places. Identifying patterns or regularities in and between these spaces is critical for understanding, theory building, and designing for spaces to support different computing activities and social influence.

If the forms and configurational features of built environments convey information, present possibilities and limitations, and influence movement and behavior, it seems that computing spaces, real or virtual, would likewise impose similar influences and constraints. If we could represent these spaces in terms of their relational components, then borrowing techniques from architecture would allow us to quantify their configurational properties and visually represent them accordingly. The ultimate goal is to amass enough data from different computing environments to begin to compare them and derive theoretical principles that may then be systematically tested.

2.3.1 Space as Object

In configuration theory, space itself is the object of analysis. In other words, the measured space— the layout or the grid—is of more interest than what is specifically in the space per se. Using various techniques, the space as an object can be quantified in different ways to predict movement, flow, and interaction. In essence, these analytic tools result in a type of pattern analysis in which the focus is on quantifying the relation among the spaces within a larger space, such as the relation between rooms within the layout of a floor plan. From this, an understanding of the whole space may be derived.

By identifying "non-discursive regularities" (Hillier, 1996), that is, spatial and formal patterns of movement, we discover what is invariant in these patterns. The goal of *configuration analysis* is to extract these invariants in order to understand the whole from the relationships among its elemental units.

In understanding these regularities or patterns, the social and cultural functions in the spaces are simultaneously revealed (Hillier, 1996). Because spatial layouts themselves convey certain information about function, there are "clear relationships between space patterns and how collections of people use them" (p. 93).

2.3.2   Affordances of Space

Configuration theory is grounded on the premise that the relationship between elements in a space contributes to the overall functioning of that space more than any one of the elements in isolation. From a cognitive/perceptual standpoint, psychologists have long concerned themselves with how humans come to recognize objects, identify visual patterns, and construct cognitive maps of their external surroundings. From the diverse literature, one can find much in common with the above basic tenet of configuration theory. For example, from a Gibsonian perspective, human perception is direct and immediate; all the information we need for perception is available in the spatial and surface layout of the immediate environment in which we find ourselves (Gibson, 1979). We make sense of what we see not through some mediating interpretive cognitive process, but by extracting invariant properties of objects and spaces (that which does not change), from the multiple perspectives from which we view it. We deduce the structure, the affordance, and the essence of a thing or space by identifying recurrent, unchanging properties (Norman, 1988). The very goal of *configurational analysis* is the detection of invariant patterns within and across spaces.

Relatedly, as Hillier points (p. 97) out, the "… human predilection for configuration …" can also be noted in the very structure of our language. Like the behavioral outcomes generated by other abstract artifacts, "The words that make up speech and behaviors that seem social are all manifested in space-time sequences of dispositions of apparent elements whose interdependencies seem to be multiplex, and irreducible to simple rules of combination." Paraphrasing from Chomsky, Hillier continues, "… that sentences … [are] a configurational proposition. Some degree of syncretic copresence of many relations is involved whose nature cannot be reduced to an additive list of pair wise relations" (p. 100).

In addition to a cognitive disposition for configuration and extraction, there is other evidence that supports the rationale for exploring configuration theory as it applies to computing behavior. The configural properties of a built environment contribute on a local level to how humans behave in them, which in turn impacts how that built environment evolves as part of a more global complex. Hillier suggests that these behaviors "… seem to be governed by *pattern* (his emphasis) laws of some kind" and that "there is a kind of natural geometry to what people do in spaces" (p. 101).

Other scholars have spent years observing people in built environments and articulating hundreds of patterns for the design of healthy and vital environments (Alexander et al., 1977; Whyte, 1988). For example, Whyte describes the use of public spaces that seem almost instinctual, unconscious, and archetypal. He was particularly interested in studying what made some places popular and others deserted. Wall sitting and carrying capacity behavior offer a fascinating account of how people self-regulate the distribution of space for sitting along a ledge, and the carrying capacity within a certain comfortable range. The role of light, warmth, and physical arrangements were a few of the factors that contributed to the success of a space. Whyte (1980, p. 19) believes that there is pleasure in seeing others and being seen by others in public spaces. One example is the fact that "what attracts people most ... is other people." Enabling people to watch the "show" of other people's movements and activities is one of the main factors for the success of a space. "The activity on the corner is a great show, and one of the best ways to make use of it is, simply, not to wall it off. A front row positions is prime space, if it is sittable, it draws the most people" (p. 57).

2.3.3   Social Navigation and Social Influence

Building in computer-mediated communication features allows for social navigation by users. A goal of social navigation is to "utilize information about other people's behavior for our own navigational decisions" (Dieberger, 1999, p. 35). Information spaces have often helped people choose appropriate information by exploiting relationships between things. Because information goals are a primary concern in museums, for example, museum technologies support semantic navigation both with low-technology artifacts such as audio tours and brochures, and in more recent systems that add multimedia content, guidebooks, personalization technologies, and other tools to supplement the standard placards of art information placed next to exhibits (Gay and Hembrooke, 2004).

Amazon.com was one of the first online companies to use a social recommendation system for identifying and suggesting books similar to the book the reader is ordering. The recommender system involves using the preferences and advice of others to help determine what is relevant about the information currently being dealt with. With context-aware computing, this information can include the user's current location, documents they are looking at, who they are with, etc. Individuals may encounter the same context at different times, but if information about these encounters can be recorded, the history of interaction can be used to inform future users and help them make decisions about their own activities (Dieberger, 1999).

One way to create these relationships is through "social navigation," or by using the activity of other individuals to make choices (Burrell et al., 2002; Gersie et al., 2003). Social navigation can be used in any networked system where multiple users are interacting with their environment, and this information can be recorded in some way and then shared. Combining social navigation with context-aware computing can result in location-mediated communication, document-mediated communication, or event-mediated communication within a program. The original idea of collectively gathering information from users and using it to influence and guide other users was inspired by research in social navigation (Dourish, 1999). Most researchers studying social navigation use these ideas to open up networked information spaces (often Web resources) to dynamic user-created content. However, it has been pointed out that we can witness social navigation both in the real and virtual worlds of information spaces (Munro et al., 1999). In the physical world, people observe the behavior of others all the time to determine where to go, what to do, or how to behave. However, without the presence of other people, or the traces they leave behind, users cannot benefit from what others have done. Cornell University researchers, for instance, have created an information space comprising user behavior and comments that are layered on top of physical space to make these traces visible for an extended period. A system that includes social maps and annotation of space with notes allows users to leave traces in a physical space that would otherwise have no record of who was present and what went on before.

2.4   DESIGNING FOR SPACE, PLACE, AND CONTEXT IN THE ART MUSEUM

2.4.1   Creating a New Museum Experience

The public art museum is an environment rich with a sense of place. Although the role of the museum is continuously debated among museum studies scholars, for the most part, the behavioral frame of the museum has remained relatively consistent. Curators and exhibit designers orchestrate the museum experience, whether for the purposes of preservation, education, and/or entertainment. Objects selected for display on the walls or on pedestals are granted the status of art. Visitors navigate through the museum encountering the objects on display and receiving cues or information on how to interpret the objects' meaning and significance through placards or tombstones. Frequently, digital technologies enter in to the art museum, and adopt a familiar role either as an object of art or as a tool, such as an audio guide, for understanding the art on display. Although technology is often used for allowing visitors a more customized experience, for instance, allowing greater visitor control in determining what information is accessed on a self-guided tour, technology design for museums rarely allows visitors to step beyond institutionally accepted behaviors, such as adopting practices of the curator or the artist.

Initial introductions of context-aware computing into museum environments underscore how technology design tends to maintain existing behaviors or existing notions of the museum as place. In early applications, context was defined as a visitor's current location and, in some implementations, the visitor's pattern of use (Marty et al., 2003; Sparacino, 2002). The digital guide, in the form of a handheld computer or even a wearable headset, monitors the visitor's position and the amount of information accessed for each piece of art. From this input, the system anticipates what information would be most appropriate to deliver next. In this example, the goal is to make the system more aware of the visitor's context, and the objective is to "optimize" the visitor's experience.

As an intended agent for change in the museum as place, the technology must be appropriated to support new behaviors: either new behaviors identified by us as designers or new behaviors imagined by visitors (Boehner, et al., 2005b). The key questions we wished to explore are: How does people's existing sense of place (their abstraction of the museum experience) influence their appropriation of technology for new activities? How might new activities supported by technology be accounted for in the museum experience? What design strategies allow for greater appropriation (i.e., transforming place) versus greater assimilation (i.e., maintaining place) of technology in museums?

However, museums serve not just as a place for information gathering, they also serve social and liminal or spiritual needs as well (Bell, 2002; Halkia and Local, 2003; Woodruff et al., 2001; Brown et al., 2003). At any given time, a museum houses not only objects but a collection of people, and the unique dynamic presence of people's activity in a museum space can dramatically influence the overall experience.

People who visit museums as part of a group experience museums differently than individuals (Ciolfi and Bannon, 2003; Heath et al., 2002; vom Lehn et al., 2007). During their visit, social groups can discuss the exhibits as a whole or each piece individually. A few systems explicitly support groups in museums. Sotto Voce (Grinter et al., 2002) provides a shared audio channel allowing pairs of visitors to communicate with one another and share experiences remotely. The Museum Detective (Boehner et al., 2005c) includes interactive activities and puzzles that children can both work on collaboratively and use to share their experiences with other children. Hornecker and Stifter (2006) suggest that museums should explicitly afford communication among groups of visitors based on their own experiences and the success of this "museum groupware."

The majority of people in a museum, however, are strangers, and little is known about how strangers affect each other's museum experiences. In prior work, we found that interactions tended to occur within preexisting groups of people such as families and tour groups, whereas direct communication across groups was not common (Boehner et al., 2005a). However, people would often overhear other people's comments, regardless of whether they attended to them; furthermore, people were influenced by the presence and activities of others (vom Lehn et al., 2007).

Guestbooks are a common communication medium between strangers in a museum. Ferris et al. (2004) used a guestbook-like feature in their work, capturing audio opinions of visitors about a collection of objects. To address issues of clearly accommodating different goals for visiting a museum, such as social, spiritual, or educational, Ferris et al. physically separated the social and learning ecologies in their application, placing learning activities in a "Study Room," and collecting and visualizing visitors' opinions in a "Room of Opinion."

2.5   CORNELL HCI RESEARCH: SOCIAL USES OF CONTEXT-AWARE COMPUTING

The Cornell University HCI Laboratory has been interested in how context-aware technology might be designed to change the museum experience, and more specifically how it might affect opportunities for social interactions and creative expression (Boehner et al., 2005c; Gay and Hembrooke, 2004; Cosley et al., 2008). Bell has critiqued museum practices for privileging the views of experts and positioning visitors as passive recipients of these expert views, thereby possibly silencing other views and interpretations (Bell, 2002). She urges designers to optimize opportunities for social interactions and engagement. She further urges designers to recognize the nature of the museum as a social place and to facilitate interactions across and among visitors.

There are many practical and theoretical arguments for enhancing sociability in museums. From a practical perspective, the decline of public funding for museums has led to an impetus for reinvigorating the experiences available to visitors, and ideally, attracting more visitors. Using technology to affect the sociability of museum spaces is not a new initiative (Finlay, 1977), and it is important to note that sociability takes on different tones in different museums, and depends on factors such as museum size, type, and visitors. Science museums, for example, tend to use technology more readily as part of an exhibit to invoke interaction with the display or with other visitors.

We have found art museums a more challenging environment for supporting sociability. One of our previous attempts, ArtView, was designed for online museums and drew from the nascent popularity at that time of chat rooms and MOOs (multi player text-based online virtual reality games) (Gay et al., 1997). In ArtView, visitors to the virtual museum created a chat channel by virtue of the picture they were simultaneously viewing with others. In comparing discussions in the ArtView environment versus discussions in the physical environment of the museum space, participants felt less inhibited in the online discussions but also found that their conversations tended to digress quickly and that the virtual representation of the art could not compare with being in the same room with it. A natural evolution of this application was to port the conversation channel of ArtView back into the physical museum, such as with MUSE, a handheld museum tour (Gay and Hembrooke, 2004).

For the past several years, researchers at the HCI Laboratory at Cornell University have been examining how context-aware technology might be designed to change experiences in public spaces, and, more specifically, how it might affect opportunities for social interaction and creative expression (Boehner et al., 2005c; Cosley et al., 2008). MUSE (Gay and Hembrooke, 2004) is a context-aware guidebook that incorporates aspects of a guestbook, including the ability to leave comments on art pieces. In initial testing, users primarily saw it as a way to ask questions of curators, rather than as a tool for connecting to other visitors. Users of another context-aware system designed for college campus tours were much more willing to interact socially and share their experiences, suggesting that in the museum, people may have been inhibited from commenting because they expected and desired expert information from the guidebook (Gay and Hembrooke, 2004).

The Imprints Project (Boehner et al., 2005e) focused on the social aspects of the museum experience, asking users to create an icon to represent themselves and attach that icon to museum exhibits. Unlike MUSE, however, Imprints represented social presence, or the activities of other viewers, in an indirect manner, which precluded explicit informational input. Imprints users were very likely to both create icons for themselves and seek out the traces (icons) of other visitors.

These findings point to the value in exploring designs that support social and liminal museum ecologies without emphasizing the learning ecology. Marrying all three ecologies would be ideal, but we have found that visitors' expectations of museum technologies are likely to lead them to focus only on the information aspects since that has been the primary use of technologies in museum spaces (Boehner et al., 2005e). Therefore, people's conceptions of places, and their resulting expectations, shape their use of technologies.

Our laboratory's previous attempts at supporting the social aspects of a museum experience have focused on providing visitors a channel for explicitly commenting on their reactions to objects (Gay et al., 1997; Gay and Hembrooke, 2004). For example, while touring the museum, visitors could use a handheld guide to leave a comment for curators or other visitors. However, we found that very few visitors used this feature despite its accessibility. In explaining the lack of use of the feature, visitors indicated that they simply did not know what to say when presented the opportunity to leave a comment. Clearly, having a channel for participation was not enough to foster participation. This finding supported Bell's (2002) critique of museums as hegemonic institutions. In other words, the predominant model in museum participation is one that encourages visitors to learn or to be entertained, but not necessarily to create and contribute. However, visitors are already implicitly commenting on the museum experience by virtue of what they choose to look at, how long they spend with certain objects, how they react to these objects, and in what activities they engage. Therefore, we attempted to create scaffolding for a new type of museum experience, one that would foster more visitor activity.

We collected dynamic measures of existing visitor behaviors, their patterns, and preferences of movement, and information access, in order to reframe this participation through ambient displays of activity, as well as provide opportunities for visitors to tag artifacts and objects (Boehner et al., 2005a; Cosley et al., 2008, 2009). This work provided the basis of another more sophisticated mobile computing application that combined a range of interaction options—interactions that fostered a range of possibilities for navigating a museum.

2.6   SOCIAL TAGGING

MobiTags (Cosley et al., 2009), a mobile iPod Touch and social tagging system developed by Cornell's HCI group, seeks to engage people with visible museum collections by examining how space and social tagging influences navigation and experience in a public space (Boehner et al., 2005b).

Art museum spaces are typically designed to encourage individuals to view art. The primary goal for designing the MobiTags program was to develop a set of navigational tools that would help people choose, encounter, and define places within the museum space, thereby emphasizing the space in addition to the art (Cosley et al., 2009). MobiTags' design integrates the social tagging of museum objects, interactive mapping, and extra information about art objects to allow visitors to make sense of and collaboratively explore the objects and artifacts on display, whether on pedestals or grouped in glass cases. Furthermore, HCI's work with MobiTags examined how data from tagged objects, and users' reactions to the art, could be used to enrich further museum visits. In short, the research examined how space and social tagging influenced navigation and experiences in a public space. The richness of information in the MobiTags environment created three domains for navigation based on Dourish and Chalmers' (1994) research (Figure 2.1, p. 30).

2.6.1   Spatial, Semantic, and Social Navigation

The Cornell HCI design team attended to three modes of navigational analysis when designing MobiTags: spatial navigation, semantic navigation, and social navigation, based on Dourish and Chalmers' (1994) research on physical and digital spaces.

When navigating through a space, people use the physical layout, the relationships between different informational objects, and their own actions and activities. MobiTags integrated social tagging of objects, interactive maps, and information about the objects into one system.

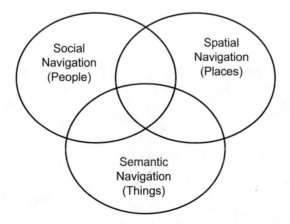

FIGURE 2.1: Social, spatial, and semantic modes of navigation. People typically use all three modes to navigate (adapted from Dourish and Chalmers, 1994).

Spatial navigation. Spatial navigation involves helping people choose, define, and reach places both online and in the physical world (Trumbull et al., 1992; Cosley et al., 2009). Much of the research in spatial navigation has looked at helping people find their way through space and the technical issues of information delivery, and how it helps users navigate through physical space (Ciavarella and Paternò, 2004; Marmasse and Schmandt, 2000).

However, providing location information indoors and out (Ciavarella and Paternò, 2004), organizing and delivering relevant information on the go (Joseph et al., 1995), and managing aspects of space affecting navigation (Troshynski, Lee and Dourish, 2008) have proven to be challenging issues for designers when building navigation tools.

To navigate through a physical or virtual space, people must use the proper tools to help them move from one area to another. Tools, for instance, could include already-established paths or maps created by others as a way to better understand the space. Over time, they could leave their own traces, impressions, or tags, thereby contributing to the navigation of others in the future.

Spaces possess both local and global elements. Local elements refer to the intricate workings within a space. In the case of MobiTags, it refers to the movement between one specific art piece and another, and the tracking system that traces the user's movements (Figure 2.2). The global element refers to the various external references that people bring to a space, including interests or knowledge that can be applied to the navigational experience. It also includes the maps and other visual organizers that help orient the user to the space.

Semantic navigation. Semantic navigation helps people move through spaces by exploiting the meanings and relationships between attributes of things (Cosley et al., 2009). Traditional museum technologies (guidebooks, audio tours, index/guide to collections, and other tools) support semantic navigation by helping people select appropriate information for learning about an object or artifact in an exhibit (Falk and Dierking, 1992). Recent computer applications allow visitors to

FIGURE 2.2: Maps in MobiTags. The left image is an overview of the subcollections. At right is the collection inside the workshop area. Selecting an object loads associated tags and information.

access and link information nonsequentially. In addition, these applications help visitors to create their own customized paths through informational material, and to annotate and personalize their tours.

Social navigation. When Dourish and Chalmers (1994) introduced the concept of social navigation, they defined it as "navigation towards a cluster of people or navigation because other people have looked at something" (p. 8). In social navigation, people watch the activity of other people to make choices about what is popular, what paths to follow, and to find links to related information (Hook et al., 2003).

Social recommender systems can help guide users through complex webs of information and subject matter by tracking the path of the users and recommending areas to explore. For example, a visitor could be looking at a painting by Andrew Wyeth and link to other paintings by Wyeth or follow popular paths based on aggregate information from visitors with similar interests.

Social navigation can potentially transform different spaces by encouraging people to explore the spaces that might otherwise be ignored or overlooked.

2.6.2   Designing for Integrated Navigation

Ideally, mobile technologies should support all three of the aforementioned forms of social navigation. Systems such as Cooltown (Fleck et al., 2002) and PEACH (Stock et al., 2007) support spatial navigation and physical orientation as well as semantic information about objects, and social recommendations about art and others' experiences.

Similarly, MobiTags' primary goal is to support social, spatial, and semantic navigation through the integration of art information, social tags contributed by the visitors, and map-based representations of the museum space (Cosley et al., 2009). Another goal of the system is to give visitors more control over their visit by encouraging them to explore various museum spaces, and to seek out more information about the pieces in hopes that these features would improve visitors' experiences while viewing objects displayed in cases in the visible storage area. The design of MobiTags allowed researchers to study how users move between different types of navigation in mobile and social systems.

MobiTags was designed as a Web-based application on an iPod Touch device using the CIYU JavaScript Library. The default view of an object provided an overview of the object's information (Figure 2.3, left). The "more info" link provided additional information, broken into sections (Figure 2.3, center). The "choose tags" button opens up an interface for using, voting on, and adding tags (Figure 2.3, right).

2.6.3   Social Tags

For the MobiTags study, researchers tracked 23 people as they used a mobile device to virtually tag art objects in the Herbert F. Johnson Museum of Art at Cornell University. The experimenters

FIGURE 2.3: An overview of the three subcollections: the current object with a given tag (left), selecting an object and bring up portrait mode (middle), and the voting on tags interface (right).

asked visitors to either vote on existing tags or create new tags associated with a piece of art on display. Using the application required little effort, so in most cases users were able to vote on or create many different tags (Figure 2.3, right). The design of the mobile device allowed for votes to take effect immediately. An update would adjust the popularity meters of tagged votes, thereby giving people immediate feedback and showing them that they contributed to the system. Users were also able to add tags using a text box with an auto-complete feature backed by tags already in the system, as suggested by Ahern et al. (2006).

Semantic aspects of tags. Research findings indicated that people liked the idea of having detailed information about each artifact or object available during their tour. They used tags as a semantic navigation tool and the list of objects to select what to visit and to see the relationships between objects and exhibits that were not captured by the physical layout (Cosley et al., 2009). For example, a person might move from case A directly to case F based on an interesting tag from another visitor.

People also reported using the tags to help them form impressions of artifacts or objects. In the summary tag cloud view, for instance, visitors tended to notice darker tags (most popular) first, but were also interested in lighter colored (less popular) tags. A few participants stated that the tags helped them think about art in novel ways and notice things that they would have overlooked without reading the tags (Cosley et al., 2009).

2.6.4   Social Navigation

Users' tags of art objects served numerous purposes in MobiTags. As previously discussed, tags contributed to semantic navigation and additional information-seeking about the content, but tags also helped to inspire user reflection about the content. Social tags helped the users consider the presence and experience of other people in the museum, and also provided a means (through tag voting) to collaboratively understand the collection. People wanted different tags at different times, and wanted to contribute tags for many reasons: to express themselves, to improve the system, and to help others navigate through the space. Participants found the act of voting on tags to be a way to express their opinion on tags added by previous visitors, and to help future visitors navigate through the collection. Interestingly, people voted tags up four times as often as they voted tags down (Cosley et al., 2009). The dominance of up-voting relative to down-voting behavior highlighted an important tension that might affect social voting systems more generally. Since only a few people actually voted others' tags down, it could be that people refrain from down-voting because they felt pressure to respect others' opinions and/or to allow the system to reflect everyone's reactions.

2.6.5   Designing for Integrated Navigation

Spatial navigation includes not only the features of the place but also the social activity that exists in a space, because it will influence how people move through and experience the space. When navigating in space, people have personal experiences that might cause them to lack awareness of others around them, or of people who passed through the space before them. As we mentioned earlier in this chapter, Erickson et al. (1999, p. 61) defines "place" as "space plus meaning" and Harrison and Dourish (1996) define it as "as space which is invested with an understanding of behavioral appropriateness, and cultural expectations" (p. 69).

Different navigational tools can help relate social and spatial navigation by providing recommendations based on proximity as well as cues about people's locations. In MobiTags, participants made extensive use of the map as a navigational tool to help them interact with the art pieces.

2.6.6   Spatial and Semantic Navigation

For analysis of MobiTag's data, visitors' movements through physical and semantic spaces were categorized as either linear or nonlinear. Linear patterns occurred when people moved from one object to the next in a linear pattern. Nonlinear patterns developed when people moved around the collection following links and suggestions from the mobile device rather than being influenced by the order of things in the physical space (Trumbull et al., 1992; Cosley et al., 2009). Furthermore, people were more likely to navigate nonlinearly in the virtual online space. This is not surprising, as spatial navigation imposes a physical cost compared to semantic navigation. Also, semantic navigation affected people's spatial navigation, leading them to move in ways not implied by the physical layout of the museum, a sentiment echoed by several participants who said MobiTags made them move with more jumps or random patterns than they might otherwise have done (Cosley et al., 2009).

The two sets of images at the top and bottom (Figures 2.4 and 2.5) show the physical and virtual paths of visitors in the museum. Images at the top demonstrate the paths of visitors who tended to navigate along museum items in physical, linear lines. In the lower set of images, linear and nonlinear paths are again demonstrated, with the images on the upper left and right exemplifying nonlinear navigation.

Many of the participants had semantic paths that looked considerably different than their physical paths, that is, they spent time in a "space" that did not correspond to their movement in the museum, and this likely changed how they experienced the physical space. In designing tools for navigating and experiencing spaces, it is important that the social aspects of exploration and the ecological aspects of navigation be taken into consideration. Designers need to understand how information is distributed throughout the people and artifacts in an environment and how that information is picked up and used by people as they navigate through a space (Cosley et al., 2009).

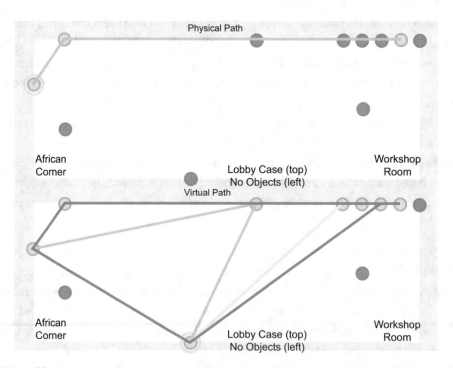

FIGURE 2.4: Top map shows linear motion and bottom map shows frequent, less linear motion through the museum.

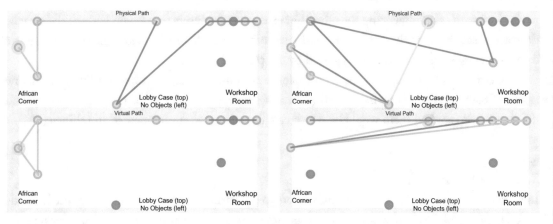

FIGURE 2.5: Images on the left show how one person's navigation through the physical and semantic spaces were quite similar. The two images on the right show that the paths were quite different.

2.7   ISSUES IN SEMANTIC, SOCIAL, AND SPATIAL NAVIGATION

As computing devices become more pervasive and ubiquitous, we find ourselves asking different questions about how to use these devices for navigation. In particular, issues such as orientation, tagging, and balancing attention all need to be considered for future designs.

Despite an almost complete lack of explicit social presence in the interface, people felt a strong sense of the presence of others through their tags in the MobiTags application (Cosley et al., 2009). In our other applications such as Imprints (Boehner, et al., 2005e) and CampusAware (Burrell et al., 2002), the programs were designed with explicit representations of other visitors that help people feel social presence. In MobiTags, the feeling of presence arose spontaneously. People reported that the mobile devices caused them to be more aware of other visitors, to be curious about what others thought, and to feel connected to others as well as to physical spaces (Cosley et al., 2008, 2009). There is value in creating a system where people can quickly and easily share thoughts with their peers, and then permit them to browse the impressions left by their group at both a high, group level and a deeper, individual level.

2.7.1   Issues Associated with Perceived Social Influence

Research findings also found that people used tags for multiple purposes: navigating, thinking about art, and creating a sense of social presence. Users valued this sense of presence, but found that it sometimes made them unwilling to evaluate other users' tags because they did not want to judge the contributions of other visitors (Cosley et al., 2009). People also interleaved spatial and semantic navigation, with each influencing the other. For example, some users focused on parts of the semantic space based on their current location, whereas others were led by semantic navigation to move through the museum in ways not suggested by the physical layout.

Designers should support these multiple ways to use tags and not necessarily privilege one aspect of tag use. When applying or voting on a tag, seeing the other items that tag applies to and the people who applied them would help to create connections between people and things (Cosley et al., 2009).

2.7.2 Local to Global Issues

In spite of the designers' best intentions, visitors to a museum still can become disoriented. In addition to being lost in a global sense within the program, users can also become lost in a local sense. Navigational problems may occur at the level of the specific paths constructed by individuals as they move using their mobile device or as they are moving through the galleries. Even though users may sufficiently understand the scope and overall design of the program to plan a general itinerary, they can become lost in the course of specific "moves," which link various navigation modes. For example, the various museum objects could have been placed on the online map that would have seamlessly linked local to global navigation.

Several problems deriving from the local context of navigation have been noted in recent research (Munro et al., 1999; Cosley et al., 2009). One example is that some users lose track of their goals. For the user whose purpose for using a particular application was initially well defined, getting distracted is both confusing and frustrating. Another example is that users are sometimes unable to return to items of information that are of particular interest. A possible solution to this would be to incorporate a tracking system into the device that would trace the user's movements through the program and space. The ability to track a user as the subject navigates through a space can help keep some individuals on track. These tracking systems may take several forms, but usually some type of visualization is available to the user showing the various paths through the program and museum. Naturally, there are privacy issues and data management issues when using any of these devices.

However, it should be noted that the very structure of these programs allowed for searching by association and for a greater possibility of serendipitous finds of pertinent information as visitors browsed through the museum spaces. In our research, we have learned that users benefit from serendipity and that many enjoy the experience of discovering unexpected pieces of information (Burrell et al., 2002; Cosley et al., 2009).

2.7.3 Quality of Contributions

When a system becomes open to contributions from all visitors, there is the risk that the information may be inaccurate or of low quality. Accuracy is an important issue for social tagging and navigation research because notes of low quality can potentially turn users off and the system can lose credibility. Although a recommendation from an expert might be more valuable to a user of a mobile navigation system, it may be more difficult to obtain that information.

Social tagging has many advantages in a mobile and social system. Apart from being low-cost, people have a number of motivations for tagging (Ames and Naaman, 2007). The steve .museum project shows that people are willing to contribute tags even though they cannot discuss art in the way experts do (Trant et al., 2007). In visible storage collections, for example, visitors' tags may, in fact, be the primary source of information about the collection since signage in such displays tends to be scant.

There are several social navigation systems that can be used to resolve accuracy issues. The useful role of moderators emerging from the general group to aid, improve, and guide the use of the system has been documented in other research (Okamura, 1994). Allowing users to vote on the usefulness of notes themselves is another possible solution to this problem. Various Web sites such as Slashdot, Amazon, and eBay provide similar capabilities.

2.8   CONCLUSION

In a world of mobile ubiquitous computing, space, navigation, and social elements lend themselves to advancing our discoveries about human computing behaviors and the interactions between real and virtual worlds. Spatial metaphors give us a vernacular for thinking about and designing spaces and also a means to represent them visually so that their underlying spatial patterns can be revealed. Movement happens in and between these virtual computing spaces, and movement patterns may set the stage for the social interaction. People are influenced by physical space as well as by the movements and activity of others.

However, the context-aware application should be used to supplement rather than replace the experience of viewing an original work of art in person or visiting a particular location. Most would agree that supplanting the real-world experience would not be an appropriate use of context-aware technology. The reciprocal relationship between context, users' goals, and activities is fundamental to the successful design and deployment of these ubiquitous tools.

·   ·   ·   ·

CHAPTER 3

Creating a Sense of Presence and Awareness with Mobile Tools

3.1 INTRODUCTION

Imagine that you are at a party and you wonder if you can join a conversation between two of your friends. However, before you welcome yourself into their space, you can ascertain through their body language how closed or open their conversation might be to a third person. You first observe their gestures, their eye movements, and their subtle changes in stance and posture. Then you look at the people around them and try to gauge their involvement, if any, with your friends. This type of social situation, where we make assessments of the social cues available before we act, occurs on a regular basis in public spaces.

We read paralinguistic cues with relatively little effort in the physical world, and if questioned, we might not even recall how we sense and respond to them. Cues are an integral part of human communication, and most people, aside from those professionally trained to project, monitor, and infer from body language, are not consciously aware of its importance in our daily lives.

Thus far, the social cues we use in physical space have not been adequately adapted to online environments. If we witness a similar conversation in an online chat room, for instance, we encounter a number of differences that make it much more difficult to evaluate, and understand the conversation. Despite our dependency on the physical and nonverbal aspects of social information for communicating, an integration of these types of cues is often overlooked in the design of digital spaces (Harrison and Dourish, 1996; Erickson and Kellogg, 2001). Designers of new tools and systems have to be aware of the complex nature of the communication process, and the use of tools and channels to facilitate communication and gain a sense of common ground (Sengers et al., 2008; Clark and Brennan, 1991).

An individual's sense of awareness regarding the events, people, and objects around him/her depends on the physical aspects of social information, or cues, that are available during an experience. Human–computer interaction (HCI) researchers are applying lessons from a number of pertinent disciplines including art, architecture, social psychology, and ecology to expand the breadth of possibilities for HCI, and increase the types of information that can be acquired for awareness

(Munro et al., 1999). In the next section, I will summarize a few key communication theories that pertain to social presence and awareness, and seek to explain how they have been applied to HCI research.

3.2   SOCIAL AWARENESS AND PRESENCE

A number of different projects have been developed in recent years that attempt to address the lack of paralinguistic cues in digital environments. Erikson's Babble interface (Erickson et al., 1999), for example, created a social proxy for these cues or signals to indicate presence, situational awareness, activity, and integration. The Babble system represents individuals engaged in a discussion as colored dots around a circle, placing individuals closer or farther away from the center based on their participation in the discussion. Furthermore, systems such as Chat Circles (Viegas and Donath, 1999), and another project involving visualizations of social turn-taking based on audio input (DiMicco et al., 2004; Kulyk et al., 2006), have demonstrated that social proxies can improve a user's awareness of other involved users, and positively influence activity. In this last case, visualizing another member's participation relative to the entire group dynamic has been shown to prompt the socially dominant contributors to become more aware of their behavior (DiMicco et al., 2004) and attempt to balance group participation (Kulyk et al., 2006). Similarly, it was found that by augmenting synchronous computer-mediated environments with visualizations of contribution levels from individual members, participants perceived the group experience as more positive and effective, and increased overall performance (Janssen et al., 2007). As demonstrated by these examples, using social proxies or cues to represent activity in many cases increased the information richness, or the "ability of information to change understanding within a time interval" (Daft and Lengle, 1984).

Those communication situations that overcome different frames of reference and clarify ambiguous issues to promote understanding in a timely manner are considered more rich, whereas those that take a longer time to convey a message are considered less rich (Daft and Lengle, 1984). The importance of information richness can also be seen in Gavers' (1992) work in the evaluation of video-based media spaces and his attention to the limited peripheral vision and perceptual exploration found in many spaces. When conferencing with someone through video, one cannot see their partner's full surroundings and does not know what or who else might be competing for his or her attention. In other words, a person's constrained field of view removes more information than they are aware of until they experience a video exchange that was disjointed due to a lack of social cues.

Researchers have used the notion of *social presence* to analyze possible uses of mobile devices. Social presence was first used by Short et al. (1976) in their teleconferencing theory by the same name, and is related to the media richness theory described above. In this theory, social presence is determined by one person's awareness of his/her social partner's presence and is determined by the capabilities of the communication medium. Generally, more contact and bandwidth are thought to increase social presence and social influence.

Social presence theory has been a divisive topic among theorists because the assumption is that full bandwidth is needed for social interactions. However, some argue that text-based forms of communication (SMS, email) are also conducive to social influence and social interaction (Walther et al., 2005).

Fulk et al. (1995) take a social constructionist view of media perception by arguing that the characteristics and utility of media, and ultimately those forms of media appropriated by individuals, is determined not by the characteristics of the medium but through social interaction with others. One's perception of media richness, therefore, is in large part a product of the overt and covert evaluations of media held by those in one's close social network, and are conveyed through interaction within and about those media.

Conversely, other scholars have argued that there are certain communication functions that cannot, in principle, be accomplished without physical copresence and the communicative signals that accompany it. For example, Nardi and Whittaker (2002) argue that face-to-face (FtF) interaction is a requisite for communication partners to be able to relate and work effectively. Some of the critical processes thwarted by mediated communication, they argue, include being able to monitor one another's attention and availability, and the ability to form an interpersonal bond.

However, other theoretical positions are also emerging. One position argues that there are certain functions and benefits of FtF interaction that are not *yet* replaceable through mediated systems, and that the cues and processes—many of which happen without conscious awareness—are not yet understood well enough to be replaceable with machine signals or routines that would allow them to function without proximity (Olson and Olson, 2001). Moreover, Clark and colleagues (Clark, 1996; Clark and Brennan, 1991; Clark and Wilkes-Gibbes, 1986) have developed a theoretical model in which successful communication relies on common ground, or the beliefs, presuppositions, and knowledge that are mutually shared by a speaker and listener. Common ground is gained when participants coordinate their activities to reach the mutual assumption that each utterance has been sufficiently comprehended by everyone for current purposes. Visual information in an FtF encounter, for example, can facilitate grounding by providing evidence about each participant's current state of activity and understanding—an understanding that some would argue is currently unattainable in computer-mediated communication (CMC), but a major goal in HCI research.

The necessity of visual and socioemotional cues, or the perception of said cues, then, lies at the heart of both FtF communication and CMC. As mentioned in the beginning of this chapter, our overfamiliarity with these cues in our daily interactions has led us to take them for granted in system design, and has resulted in a significant discrepancy between the two forms. Moreover, without the appropriate cues-based information, many digital systems fail outright unless users can recreate the needed cues themselves. This adaptation is evidenced in the rise of the user-generated emoticon, which eventually went on to be appropriated by designers and integrated into computing systems as an essential form of CMC.

Therefore, designers of digital systems must encourage an experience that is meaningful by emphasizing presence, or perceived presence, a sense of realism, transportation, and immersion (Lombard and Ditton, 1997). The role of the social actor within the medium, the role of the medium as social actor, and the social richness, all of which regard presence as the "perceptual illusion of non-mediation," play an equally important role in improving a sense of person-perception. For example, early experiments with video media spaces attempted to use video in users' offices and in common areas to support mutual awareness and informal communication (Gavers, 1992; Finn et al., 1977). In these systems, users could see video images of remote colleagues in their offices, and use the visual information to assess user availability and to initiate interaction.

In the next section, I will describe how HCI researchers and designers have been implementing these theories to attempt to increase awareness and social presence using mobile computing tools.

3.3   AMBIENT DISPLAYS OF PRESENCE

One of the recent goals of HCI designers has been to incorporate social awareness and interaction into physical spaces via ambient displays. One of the main goals of ambient displays is to connect information that exists in the "periphery" or in the edge of our awareness to foreground activity (Boehner et al., 2005c).

In conceptualizing a system for displaying peripheral social information, research has looked to the growing body of work in ambient displays or peripheral digital information that can be embedded into the objects in our surrounding environment (Iishi, 2006). These digital displays can be in the form of light, motion, sound, and other media that exist in the periphery of our senses where they provide continuous information without being distracting. This ambient display information is "peripheral" in the sense that it is separate and discrete from other activities (Boehner et al., 2005c).

Ambient displays provide continuous information to individual users and help foster awareness without demanding one's full attention. For example, a person is working on a report in the office. In this situation, typing and concentrating exist as his/her foreground activities. Meanwhile, a peripheral display of, say, traffic density in his/her neighborhood could be ambiently displayed in the form of a glowing orb, and sits upon his/her desk, displaying a gradation of colors that represent a variety of local traffic situations as he/she begins to think about the evening commute. The display itself is not in any way associated with producing his/her report, but it flickers away, unobtrusively communicating environmental information to him/her peripherally. However, with even a brief glance in the direction of the orb, the device is drawn out of the periphery and into momentary direct attention of the person, who then gets a sense of local traffic conditions as he/she finishes his/her report and prepares to drive home.

Moving beyond the individual, ambient displays can also influence and highlight existing patterns of navigation in physical spaces with large numbers of people. In many public spaces, people attend to the presence of others without any formal training or direction (Galani and Chalmers, 2004). For example, the arguable center of Cornell's sprawling campus is Ho Plaza, a pedestrian thoroughfare connecting Ithaca's collegetown to the university. On any given day in Ho Plaza, thousands of students pass through on their way to and from campus and come across countless social situations that they choose to encounter or ignore. They seamlessly navigate around each other while catching snippets of others' conversations, and glances from others' eyes. While some students stand around and catch up in-between classes, others move through the plaza, hardly taking notice of their surroundings.

In public situations, individuals have an implicit sense of presence, but an explicit acknowledgment of that sense is never guaranteed. For this reason, ambient displays can be used to draw attention to this sense of awareness (Boehner et al., 2005a). For example, by creating a visual display that builds up patterns of traffic through Ho Plaza over time, pedestrians could reflect on their navigation through the space when compared to the paths of others.

In the two examples below, the spatial layout of a museum provides a familiar backdrop for the display of navigational information. In Figure 3.1, additional levels of spatial information have been made available to museum visitors beyond the traditional "you are here" map. In addition to the location of rooms and objects, the display indicates the location and density of people and their paths through space, recommended navigational paths, and popular art works. The advantage to this type of space- and place-based knowledge is understood when a museum patron wonders why one area of the museum remains undiscovered, and thus sets off to explore the seemingly "undiscovered" space. In addition, one has the opportunity to, for instance, trace the same path of an anonymous stranger and wonder what connections he or she made between various objects. Furthermore, visitors can consult their handheld map to not only see where their favorite painting is located, but to see the number of people looking at it at that moment (Figure 3.2) or if it has attracted a number of other visitors throughout the day. By building up traces of foot traffic as a form of collaborative filtering, we can build impressions of popular, nonpopular, or undiscovered areas of the museum (Figure 3.1).

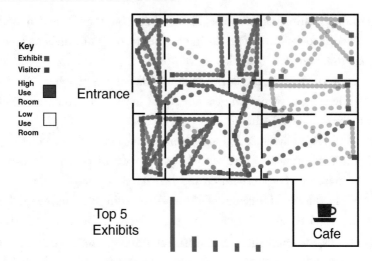

FIGURE 3.1: A visual display of visitors' traffic patterns over time.

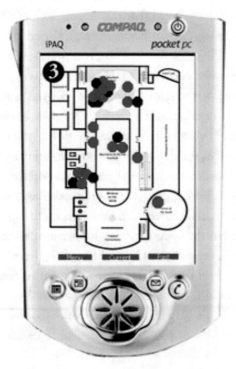

FIGURE 3.2: Numbers of visitors viewing objects or artifacts in a museum.

3.4   EMOTIONAL CLIMATE AND AFFECTIVE AWARENESS

We unconsciously monitor our surrounding physical environment, and the people that occupy those spaces. Phrases such as "the atmosphere in the room changed" or "the place was bursting with enthusiasm" suggest the ability, or at least the perception of the ability, to read a situation for context cues of collective emotional states and activity. Much of the work in affective computing focuses on ways in which computers can become aware of, and process data about, these human emotional states (Picard, 1997; Ark et al., 1999; Ortony et al., 1988; Fernandez et al., 1999).

Building technologies for sharing mood or emotional reactions is not new. However, there are few designs that allow users to share their own moods or enhance their social awareness of others. In this section, we will briefly examine applications and work being conducted in mood sharing technologies.

MoodJam, created at the Human Computer Interaction Institute at Carnegie Mellon University, is a Web-based application that provides users with a palette of colors from which they can choose one to best reflect their mood. Additionally, the user can supplement their color selections with words or notes and post the selection to "Your Moods," a publicly available site. Visitors to the site can mouse over colors and see comments or tags.

MoodJam gives the user the option of choosing the colors that best suit his or her emotional state. LinkMood is another Web-based application that allows users to choose from an extensive list of words to let others know how they are feeling, and also provides a short space for users to leave a short note or description to talk about why they are in the mood they are in. Furthermore, moods are archived so users can track how their moods have changed over time.

The HCI Lab at Cornell has developed a mobile application called Aurora, using the MoodJam application as a model (Figure 3.3). Aurora (Gay et al., 2009) encourages patients to share their current mood and comfort levels with one another via a simple interface. At any time, users can log into the system and choose graphics, photos, or colors to represent their current mood or emotional state, rate their current comfort levels, and provide a short textual description of their status similar to away messages or status messages in other popular online social applications. Users are always able to see the current mood, comfort, and status message of other members of their social group, as well as an aggregate mood and comfort display for the entire population of users. In addition, users are able to easily send text messages to one another through the interface (Gay et al., 2009).

In addition to MoodJam and Aurora, several mobile applications have examined the use of affective computing in context. One such project is Connecto, a mobile location-sharing application. Although the researchers set out to gain a better understanding of how users might apply location sharing and location awareness to improve coordination and foster social connection, they discovered that the system was instead largely used for the sharing of mood and emotional status (Barkhuus et al., 2008).

FIGURE 3.3: The Aurora mobile application is used for sharing emotional states with others. Users select a color or an image and attach a message to the image. Users can also view others' images and send messages to them.

Another museum application, based on movement, activity, and density, took the form of an "emotional climate map" (Figure 3.4). Color-coding areas of the museum floor plan suggested different "atmospheres" in various regions of the gallery (Boehner et al., 2005d).

Finally, users of the eMoto mobile system carry with them a special stylus fitted with pressure sensors and an accelerometer. When sending a text message to another user of the system, the user

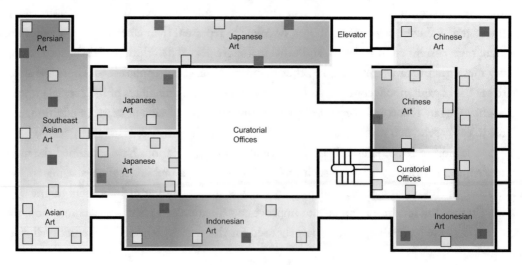

FIGURE 3.4: Emotional climate map of another museum space.

squeezes and shakes the stylus in a manner befitting their mood. The eMoto device recognizes these actions through the sensors in the stylus and uses an algorithm to generate a background image for their text message composed of colors and shapes. Users can alter the pressure applied to the stylus and their movements to generate an image they find consistent with their mood (Sundström et al., 2007).

In sum, mobile applications should cause reflection on social presence, and create greater awareness and interaction with a space. Applications should also be open to interpretation (eg, the primary goal is to have people reflect on social presence and create greater awareness, but they may reflect on other things such as computer surveillance, privacy, using social recommender systems to change visitors' experiences). Additionally, applications should be enjoyable and engaging. In many of these system, the user had the ability to select a representation for their mood without too much effort or interpretation, and the resulting representation had enough ambiguity to allow for creative representations and interpretations, but not so much that the user would feel that what they are sharing will have no meaning to other users (Sengers et al., 2008).

3.5   CREATING A SENSE OF PRESENCE

Recently, there have been a number of research studies aimed at figuring out ways to encourage online contribution and participation. Researchers have looked at the problem of motivating users to contribute, particularly in online support groups (Maloney-Krichmar and Preece, 2005), and Wikipedia (Cosley et al., 2005). To critically engage users with these systems, researchers must take a sociological perspective: *What motivates users to contribute to digital content, and how can researchers shape participation?*

One problem results from the "disparity between those who will benefit from an application and those who must do additional work to support it" (Grudin, 1990). Alan Cooper calls this the principle of commensurate effort, which states that users are willing to work harder when they feel they will be rewarded, or that they will work hard when they think their effort will help them achieve outcomes they value (Cooper, 1999; Karau and Williams, 2001). In support of this argument, Dieberger (1999) notes that in social navigation systems where users share information to guide each other, a virtual community consisting only of consumers will not be successful, and that when they are short on time or competing against each other, users may be unwilling to contribute (Cooper, 1999). Furthermore, when users are reluctant to compete against each people, short on time, or feel that others may be critical of their comments, they may be unwilling to contribute (Dieberger, 1999).

3.6   CAMPUS AWARE APPLICATION: SOCIAL MAPPING OF SPACE

We witness social navigation both in the real world and in the virtual worlds of information spaces (Munro et al., 1999). In the physical world, people constantly observe the behavior of others to determine where to go or what to do. As previously mentioned, you see this every time people move as a crowd, follow along the worn path of a hiking trail, or even follow someone's gaze to see what they are looking at. However, without the presence of other people or the traces they leave behind, users cannot benefit from what others have done.

Traces of one's experiences can take many forms in both the digital and physical realms. Physical traces tend to be indexical in nature, that is, they remain as visible or tangible "proof" of one's experience (Messaris, 1997). For example, the outline of a hand pressed into a cement sidewalk indicates to passersby that at one time an individual his/her hand into the wet cement, thereby leaving a visible trace of the event. Other examples include footprints in the mud, graffiti on a wall, or an echo in a tunnel. These types of traces are common indicators of presence. However, not all traces of experience or presence are so evident, as they may also exist in nontangible forms.

As individuals navigate through space and interact with the people and objects in that space, they begin to accumulate memories of their encounters. As a result, they may begin to place more value on those places (Canter, 1977). In a public space, people carry with them the stories and memories that they form there, especially if the movements are repeated over time (Seamon, 1979). Moving through space, then, means to move through a myriad of memories made by other people who have also navigated through the space. Thus, spatial navigation is not a mindless activity that involves people blankly moving from one space to another. Even though there are many times when a person may not be consciously aware of his/her surroundings, he or she, in fact, in still subconsciously collecting the information that is occurring around him or her (Jung, 1964).

If a person is encouraged to be more aware of his or her movements in space, navigation and place-making can be reflexive experiences that involve the observation of and reflection upon his or her surroundings. Investigating the link between memory and place, Castrenze (2008) used autobiographical narrative and audio recordings to document the sounds and personal memories associated with specific places in his life. In this case, sound functioned as an element of context, where the sounds were, according to Dey (2001), pieces of information "considered relevant to the interaction between a user and an application" (p. 4). Sounds and memories associated with a place can help researchers understand the dynamic relationships that occur in space because they indicate some of the different social, cultural, spatial, and temporal factors involved (Castrenze, 2008; Truax, 2001). For instance, the hourly chime of Cornell's McGraw clock tower not only indicates the time of day to students below, but also helps convey a sense of space that is dependent on an individual's distance from the tower. Furthermore, the chimes also represent the cultural traditions of the university as well as the social conditions within which the student body operates. If a former student returns to the clock tower decades later and hears the same chimes, he may remember the feelings that were first felt when he was a student, and a flood of memories might come back to him, instantly re-placing him in the space.

Through the process of recording memories and observing physical traces, people can increase their awareness about the presence of others in a space. However, other traces of presence can be more accurately expressed in a digital format such as Cornell HCI's Campus Aware system.

Campus Aware sought to help individuals understand the traces of others on Cornell's campus by creating a digital information space that depicted the patterns of the application's users, and then layered the resulting data on top of a map of Cornell's campus. By using a handheld device, users were able to observe the paths of other individuals while also detailing their experiences with the space around them.

Our research on incorporating user behavior and knowledge into a context-aware system began in 2000, when we started exploring a system called E-Graffiti that allowed users to create text messages and attach those messages to a location where anyone could read them (Burrell et al., 2002). Because this was a relatively new technology at the time, a number of usability problems emerged in the evaluation phase. For example, users were misinterpreting the intent of the system and transforming it into a synchronous chatting system while ignoring all of the context-awareness functionality.

In our next design called Campus Aware (Burrell et al., 2002), we envisioned an unobtrusive guide to the physical environment, and one that provided information to the user only when it was relevant and novel. Our philosophy was that the primary experience of the user revolved around viewing and experiencing the physical campus, and that our system should play only a supporting role.

Our primary research goal for Campus Aware was to make a simple and reliable system that would allow us to investigate some of the usability problems unique to the area of context-aware computing. Furthermore, we sought to develop a tool to help visualize the social activities and resulting impressions that form in spaces and places. Therefore, the design had to emphasize context awareness while also encouraging users to create content (Burrell et al., 2002).

3.6.1   Mobile Social Media in Physical Spaces: Opportunities and Issues

Looking at the actual design and format of Campus Aware, the colored mood indicators and comments were intended to promote reflection upon the identity and presence of other individuals who had also been in that same space (Figure 3.5). They were also meant to stimulate questions about the user's reactions to the spaces during navigation throughout the campus. For instance, while operating the device, people could click on the tags to gather or create new information. This provided users the opportunity to create content for the system. Anyone who used the application was able to annotate, or tag a physical location on the map as it correlated with the surrounding physical space.

The issues surrounding user's reactions to Campus Aware have been broken down into three areas that attend to the integration of social media into physical spaces. These themes and issues are

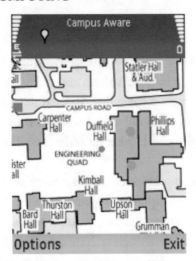

FIGURE 3.5: Screen shot of Campus Aware cell phone application. Colored dots and squares indicate areas where users have posted comments.

derived from a number of our studies of context-aware computing (Burrell and Gay, 2001, 2002; Burrell et al., 2002). The first area concerns the social affordances of the system. The second area concerns the balancing of attention while using the system, and the third area addresses the quality of the user's contributions.

3.6.2   Social Affordances

Campus Aware had the ability to bring together information from a number of individuals and present it at the time it was being gathered. It could also store the data to be processed at a later time. The map (Figure 3.5) took aggregated user behavior, or simple user feedback such as voting on the desirability of various campus locations, and plotted this information onto corresponding points on the map. Simple social mapping systems as part of a tour guide application helped users obtain interesting information. These social maps were presented to users and provided dynamic feedback at a point and time when people need the information. Displays such as these can be used in different public spaces, such as museums and offices, to encourage reflection and conversation on collective or aggregate movement, activity, and emotion (Figure 3.6).

We believe that systems with a social element are often much more dynamic than their nonsocial counterparts, and offer a better reflection of user concerns. Putting user-created content in a tour guide can result in a more authentic reflection of the space that is being toured. This is particularly true when visitors represent a cross section of individuals with different relationships to the space including both space experts and novices. The opportunity to present expert and novice information ties into context-aware computing because the people who regularly visit a space pre-

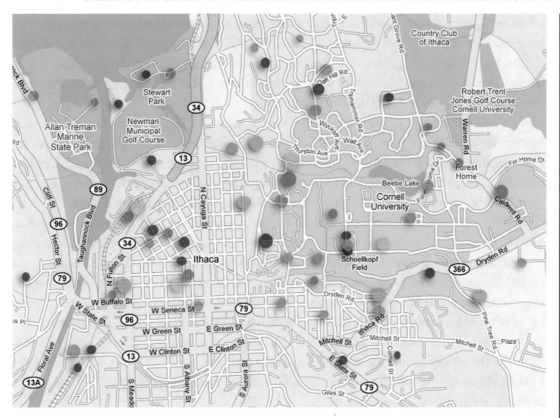

FIGURE 3.6: A social map of the campus; each dot represents a visitor's impression of a specific location. Visitors' comments are linked to each of the dots. Other visitors may leave their annotations or click on a dot to read a comment.

sumably know more about how and when the space gets used and who inhabits it when compared to those who infrequently visit the same space. What the aforementioned "experts" say in and about the space reflects a formal or informal understanding of their accumulated experiences. User-created content gives users more power over the system, allowing them to steer its use toward their own needs and interests. Systems that provide these capabilities allow people to collectively construct a range of resources that were too difficult or expensive or simply impossible to provide before (Burrell and Gay, 2001, 2002; Cosley et al., 2008).

3.6.3 Balancing Attention

Ubiquitous computing systems, whether a Global Positioning System (GPS) system in a car or a mobile phone guide, are generally designed to support interactions with the physical world. However, once a computing device is added to the environment, the individual user can no longer exclusively attend to the environment. Users must balance their attention, consciously or unconsciously, in every experience. Ubiquitous devices such as cell phones using GPS or map programs as well as more traditional forms of mediated guides, such as printed guidebooks, maps, or tours, can potentially help or hinder visitors as they strive to interact with the environment and while also using the guide. Obviously, any device or guide should not be a distraction.

In our research, we have implemented several features in Campus Aware that strive toward maintaining a balance of users' attention. For instance, in our first iteration the interface was designed with an audio alert to notify the user when a relevant note became available to read. The idea behind this design component was that a user would put the mobile device in his or her pocket and use it like a beeper, only viewing the interface when there was something new to read (Burrell et al., 2002). We also explored options for using audio rather than visual interfaces so that users' attention could be more focused on their external environment rather than the visual interface of the device.

Because we were attempting to achieve a balance between viewing the device and viewing the environment, we decided to design an aggregate visualization of the all the visitors' comments and impressions and points of interest on the map so that the user could easily use the device with devoting all of his or her attention to it. Visitors could then walk to a particular point of interest and read the notes or add their own annotations. These visualizations are similar to the abstract representations of social activity such as the aforementioned Babble (Erickson et al., 1999), and Groupmeter, a graphical interface for synchronous group communication that conveys contributions and activity in an abstract manner (Leshed et al., 2007).

3.6.4   Quality of Contributions

People had strong expectations about the role of technology in a campus tour and its use as an information appliance. Because of the map interface, people expected Campus Aware to provide information about navigation, information about the space around them, and what to visit. Even after they realized its goal was social, making connections to the space and other people, and found value in that goal, they also stated that they wanted other more factual information provided (Burrell et al., 2002; Cosley et al., 2008).

We have found in our studies that the content users tend to contribute is likely to be qualitatively different from the factual information an institution such as a museum or university administration would develop (Boehner et al., 2005a; Cosley et al., 2008). Sometimes, the social, expressive, and subversive qualities of content created by users may be more interesting than content created by administrators, which tends to be more factual and utility-oriented (Gay and Hembrooke, 2002). Therefore, opening up a system to user contributions holds the promise of content that is much more informal, opinionated, and possibly even subversive than content provided by an official source (Burrell et al., 2002; Cosley et al., 2008). Our evaluation of the types of notes users contributed demonstrates that this holds true with the Campus Aware system. However, do users value reading other users' tags?

Overall, survey responses from our various studies show that many users do value the informal, opinionated, and even humorous information posted by other users. Visitors appreciated reading annotations contributed by unofficial sources such as those from students. Furthermore, visitors felt that the unofficial notes were more "honest" and were sometimes valued more than the official factual notes that were posted.

However, although participants appreciated and valued the notes left by other visitors, almost all stated that they wanted more official background information and expert opinions or, at the very least, some means of identifying official contributions.

Incorporating user-contributed information into a location-based tour application is a valid way to generate useful tags or annotate a particular location. In our studies, we found that visitors were willing to contribute their knowledge and also found value in the content created through this process. Similarly, when users posted inaccurate information, other users posted corrections, and when users posted questions, other users also answered them.

We found that participants were concerned with the role of "experts" in context-aware environments. Most visitors to the museums and campus wanted more information about the identity of the contributors. Participants suggested that the design of the note systems could be improved if the experts' comments were displayed, for example, in bold or in a different color from the surrounding text in order to provide them with greater "visual authority." This type of change to the design could potentially help distinguish the "experts" from the "novices." Although they liked that anyone using the system could contribute notes, many suggested that experts could help keep people focused. However, there are trade-offs with any approach to knowledge dissemination.

Accuracy is an area of concern for social navigation research, and although recommendation from an expert might be more useful because one can be sure the information is correct, it may be harder to obtain that information (Dieberger, 1999). Similarly, when a system becomes open to general comments from users there is the risk that information may be obscured. Our systems rely heavily on user contributions, and, for obvious reasons, people were worried about the credibility of the information from others as well as the trustworthiness of the sources of the information.

In a number of responses, users commented on how pointless some of the annotations and tags were. It was difficult to determine whether the notes that users posted were of high quality unless someone was assigned to moderate the content. However, even with a content moderator, issues pertaining to subjective judgment and censorship arise. Notes that are commonly deemed to be low quality, if there are enough of them, can potentially turn users off from a system. Allowing users to vote on the usefulness of notes themselves is a possible solution to this problem (Cosley et al., 2009). Various websites such as Amazon and eBay provide similar capabilities. Our findings on accuracy have shown that users were willing to play the role of moderator and were likely to use this note-voting functionality (Burrell et al., 2002; Cosley et al. 2009).

Campus Aware users also requested that the program give them information pertaining to "related spots," "history of the location," "a before and after view," and "something specific to learn" (Burrell et al., 2002; Burrell and Gay, 2001). Most people seemed to want some type of combination of official and unofficial comments but almost all commented that the visualizations helped them realize that social connections were a valuable part of their experience (Burrell et al., 2002; Cosley et al., 2009). A balance between top-down and bottom-up approaches, where top-down describes the expert-based knowledge and bottom-up describes the novice-based knowledge, might work best for a more balanced Campus Aware project.

For example, when the context was relevant, users' responses were generally very positive, as indicated by their motivation to interact with other users and provide information to the system. Content analysis of the information left by users indicated that they liked this functionality, they enjoyed more informal contributions to the system, versus "official" information posted by administrators, and that much of the motivation for contributing to the system was almost driven by a sense of "duty," to inform other users of necessary information (Burrell et al., 2002).

Visitors found value in information posted by others, so there was also a payoff for them. They also seemed to have benefited from feelings of altruism and expertise resulting from contributing notes to help out others. The self-maintaining nature of our system is encouragement for designers of similar systems who are concerned about the quality, quantity, and accuracy of unmoderated content created by users.

Primary among the findings from our studies was that the notion of aware technology affiliated with activities in a particular location is ambiguous for most users, and unless the context is highly specific, users have a hard time understanding the relevancy of the functionality, and do not use it (Burrell and Gay, 2002; Burrell et al., 2002). However, as interactions on the Web have evolved from a one-way information push to interactive information-seeking and online social interactions, we are also seeing similar trends in mobile computing contexts. Services and tools for sharing, recording, and distributing social information will become more common.

3.7   CONCLUSION

In Campus Aware, we drew influences from two varieties of context-aware computing. From the "context as content" approach, we provided contextual information to visitors; however, this information was not only that of the artifacts or objects around them, but also of the social and emotional activity in the physical space (Boehner et al., 2005c; Burrell et al., 2002). In doing so, we hoped to encourage an increased sense of awareness for the users. The content we presented or reflected back to the users detailed their own personal usage patterns, as well as the presence and patterns of those around them or even those of past visitors (Boehner et al., 2005d).

By inviting visitors to see connections with others through social maps, and encouraging them to vote on one another's comments and social locations, users were encouraged to think more about their relationships to other visitors as well as the physical, cultural, and digital landscapes. By foregrounding the impressions of others, visitors gave their own impressions of the location or object more explicit consideration.

In all of our studies, we found that displaying visitors' reactions to a space through aggregate visualizations had a positive effect on how people perceived social aspects of the museum or an outdoor space. A number of informants reported that the visualization caused them to be more aware of other visitors, to be curious about what others thought, to feel connections to other people, and to like the idea of being connected to them (Burrell et al., 2002).

This chapter began with the objective of supporting place-making activities, and following along the lines of Harrison and Dourish (1996), designing for place rather than attempting to design place itself. Our research interests, therefore, have revolved around how people would appropriate this mobile technology designed for activities traditionally not supported by technology.

We were not asking people to drastically adopt new activities but instead were augmenting activities they already engaged in such as reflecting on a place during a tour of a space. By reflecting an impression or the feelings about a location, we hoped that we would enhance the visitor's engagement with a particular object, space, or with other people.

Overall, however, by showing traces of presence and activity, we were explicitly drawing attention to people's implicit understanding of the campus as a social place and a shared experience.

·   ·   ·   ·

CHAPTER 4

Mobile Computing: A Tool for Social Influence to Change Behavior

4.1 INTRODUCTION

It is springtime and a young woman wants to purchase seeds for her garden, but before she makes the purchase, she sends an email to a friend and asks for some advice about purchasing seeds. Accompanying her email is a sidebar on the right-hand side of the computer screen advertising a variety of gardening products that are sold at some nearby gardening centers. The relevance of the advertisements is no coincidence. The product messages derive from keywords extracted from her email, and the hope of the advertisers is that she, as a message-maker and a consumer, will be influenced by the ads and will purchase some of the suggested products.

With advancements in computing technology in recent years, this type of advertising, or persuasion, is becoming increasingly prevalent. In addition to distributing messages through traditional media outlets such as magazines, newspapers, or television, companies are now able to track consumer interests and behavior, and target messages directly to them through blogs, emails, or pop-up ads on the Web.

Much of the early research on media-based persuasion has focused on one-way messages and their effects on receivers (Hovland et al., 1949; O'Keefe, 2002). On the other hand, Eckles (2007) asserts that when considering persuasion in the context of today's mobile technologies, the units of analysis and definition of success are different. Rather than simple, one-way messages, "the units of persuasion are now dialogs, or ongoing interactions between the individual and the sender of the messages" (Eckles, 2007, p. 145). In the case of the email advertising scenario previously mentioned, one type of dialog involves the interactivity between the consumer and the advertisers. The consumer cannot choose whether they see the advertisements because that specific design is built into the model of the application, but the content of the advertisements that they do see is dependent on the messages they create.

As another example of dialog, let us assume that our springtime gardener visits the online sites of a few of the stores that are advertised in her emails. When she is visiting the sites, she looks for the products that she is interested in. Afterward, she formulates questions about those products and she poses them to her friend via email, and even posts them on a gardening discussion board.

From this last example, it is clear that marketers and advertisers are not the only ones that can now benefit from context-based persuasion. Users can use the Web to influence others, and the potential for this type of interaction requires a new model of persuasive communication: a model that views meaning as interactive and coconstructed (Boehner et al., 2005c; Eckles, 2007). In other words, meaning is not transferred from one individual through a channel to another individual, as portrayed by Shannon (1948), but rather, meaning develops interactively as individuals actively and jointly use various channels to construct meaning. Thus, people can influence or persuade others in their physical or virtual social networks to coordinate different meanings and interpretations of the original message to adopt some change. The end result is that the original persuasive message can be reinterpreted in a number of ways. It is crucial to realize that an individual's pattern of social relationships and interactions determines how they ultimately interpret and internalize the persuasive messages they have received (Yuan and Gay, 2006). It is often "interpersonal influence with friends and neighbors which leads to actual adoption" (Valente, 1996, p. 80). Although direct interpersonal exposure to innovation generally increases the likelihood of adoption, properties of communication networks can further enhance of the persuasive power of interpersonal exposure to an innovation (Figure 4.1). Communication networks consist of cohesion, tie homophily, and ties to opinion leaders (Rogers, 2003; Strang and Soule, 1998).

Another example that demonstrates the persuasive potential of new media can be found in mobile technology. Fogg (2002) developed the concept of the "kairos factor," which he describes as the mobile phone's potential ability to deliver the perfect persuasive message at the most opportune time. Currently, the average mobile phone user can take notes, store and look up their schedule,

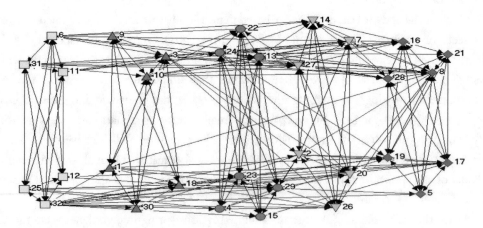

FIGURE 4.1: Social map showing connections between various distributed groups. People tended to affiliate and be persuaded by friends and people similar to themselves (Yuan and Gay, 2006).

connect to the Internet, play music, take pictures, and text their friends. Many phones are even equipped to indicate the precise location of the user as well as their activity.

Given the wealth of knowledge a mobile phone can store about its owner, and the fact that it is almost always switched on, persuasive messages could be personalized based on inferred individual traits and habits. These messages can be delivered at just the right moment based on the user's current location, time, and even the user's stored schedule. These potential factors also contribute to what Fogg (2002) viewed as the highly personal nature of the mobile phone; Fogg has even gone so far as to use the term "marriage" when describing an individual's relationship with their mobile phone. The fact that the mobile phone is always connected, and in many cases has constant access to the Internet, could give the user confidence that the quality and relevance of the information received in these messages is very high. Were this consistently the case, Fogg posits that information received from the device would be deemed to be not only of high quality but also trustworthy and useful (Fogg, 2002). The nature of the mobile phone as a constant companion, coupled with the increasing level of location-aware capabilities of these phones, makes them the perfect instrument for the delivery of persuasive messages at opportune times.

Mobile phones can be our trusted companions, confidants, guides, assistants, and potentially through the applications of persuasive technology, our coaches and mentors (Fogg and Eckles, 2007). Thus, these uses of mobile technology can shape how we interpret and act in our contexts. To further understand how mobile devices can be used as effective tools for persuasion and influence, we look to the burgeoning field of *persuasive technology*, which seeks to understand how technology can be used to change behavior through a variety of techniques borne of classic psychology and social psychology literature. Fogg (2002) has detailed numerous methods through which technology can be used to facilitate changes in behavior and connects them with theory with which to justify those methods. In particular, intrinsic motivation, social facilitation, social comparison, and social cognition and modeling are invoked as mechanisms through which technology can bring about changes in behavior.

4.2   SOCIAL INFLUENCE

Hovland and colleagues at Yale University studied the effects of different types of media and communication on attitude change (Hovland et al., 1949, 1953). In their early studies, they looked at how the process of persuasion was affected by variations in three main communication-based categories: the communicator, the audience, and the communication itself. For the communicator, they looked at credibility and the amount of change advocated; for the audience, they looked at audience personality, strength of group affiliations, and salience; and for the communication itself, they looked at its one-sidedness, the type of incentive it appeals to, and the explicitness of the message.

As noted earlier, this early model of how communication can be used to persuade has been revised to help understand joint construction of meaning. There are many factors that determine how one person can be persuaded or influenced by another. The following theories and studies describe some of the attributes that lead to cooperative or competitive interactions, the consequences of those relationships in a social context, and how they may affect individuals and their experiences.

4.2.1   Social Facilitation

One type of social influence is social facilitation (Zajonc, 1965). Social facilitation asserts that individuals are more likely to perform simple or well-learned behaviors if they believe that their behavior is being observed (O'Keefe, 2002). A common interpretation of social facilitation is that individuals will perform better if they are surrounded by others performing similar tasks, and if those other people are slightly better at performing the task than they are. Bandura and Walters (1963) were among the early researchers of social facilitation, and through their studies, found that behavioral imitation and response patterns could be acquired through observation. Social cognition and modeling (Bandura, 1986, 1997) are also frequently referenced in persuasive technology contexts as a means of encouraging positive behavior. By observing other individuals behaving in a certain manner and receiving some type of recognition or reward for that behavior, an individual is more likely to adopt that behavior for themselves, particularly when the individuals being observed are similar or identifiable.

Some researchers also believe that an individual simply perceiving that their behavior is being monitored, even by a computer system or device, will improve performance or behavior. In a persuasive technology context, social facilitation can be supported through message boards, buddy lists, and other simple representations that let users know that others are logged in and participating, and that their participation is being observed. Fogg (2002) applies this phenomenon to the technology domain by showing that individuals also model behavior when observing the actions of others through a computer, or even when observing the actions of an avatar or character in a computer environment.

It should be noted that social facilitation is different than cooperation. Under the concept of social facilitation, individuals are not necessarily working toward a common goal but are simply performing the same tasks.

4.2.2   Social Comparison

In his initial theory of social comparison, Festinger's (1954) assumption was that people are driven to find out whether their opinions are judged to be correct. Festinger also assumed that this drive produces behavior in people directed toward obtaining an accurate appraisal of their own abilities. This drive to compare one's opinion and abilities with others may lead one to change them so as to make them closer to the opinions or abilities of others who are available for comparison.

Festinger hypothesized several things. First, he stated that individuals seek out information on how they are performing relative to others around them, and then adjust their own behavior accordingly. Second, the tendency to compare oneself with some other specific person decreases as the difference between that person's opinion or ability, and one's own widens. Third, there is an upward drive toward comparing oneself to people who are deemed socially superior, showing similarities between themselves and the comparison group (Festinger, 1954). Downward social comparison, evaluating oneself in comparison to people who are worse off, tends to make people feel better and their troubles seem smaller (Suls et al., 2002).

Social comparison theory is different from competition in that it does not imply that individuals will improve their performance in order to surpass another individual; rather, they will modify their performance (either positively or negatively) to be more in line with others.

Festinger's theory of social comparison was adapted by Schachter (1959) to apply to the evaluation of emotions as well as to opinions and abilities. In his classic studies, he demonstrated that the tendency to affiliate with others undergoing a similar experience increased when subjects were made anxious. Schachter's explanation for this finding was that subjects were unclear about the appropriateness of their anxiety to the situation; hence, they desired to be with others undergoing a similar experience in order to compare their reactions. He proposes that the emotions experienced by an individual are very much influenced by the process of social comparison.

Schachter also theorized that a state of physiological arousal may be experienced as either euphoria or anger, depending on how it is interpreted, and how it is interpreted may in turn depend on the social cues derived from the behavior of others. In another series of experiments, Schachter and Singer (1962) found that subjects may interpret a given physiological arousal to make it compatible with the emotions being expressed by others in the same situation.

Festinger's theory of cognitive dissonance (Festinger, 1957) is also an extension of the theory of social comparison and the studies of emotion. Dissonance theory details the need to have actions consistent with one's knowledge and beliefs. This theory is similar to other theories that posit that people will actually change their beliefs to fit their actual behavior.

Social comparison has been shown to play an important role in the persuasion and motivation of behavior change. Countless studies, some involving technologies and some not, have shown that individuals grouped with peers have better results in quitting drinking, quitting smoking, losing weight, exercising, and even surviving cancer (Fogg, 2008).

4.2.3   Motivation

Lewin's motivational concepts are concerned with purposes and goals that lead to behavior. Lewin used the concepts *tension, force, valence,* and *locomotion* in his model of motivation. Lewin (1938) believed that a state of tension exists within a person whenever a psychological need or intention exists. Tension is released when the need is fulfilled or the objective is met. In some ways, Lewin's work relates to *activity theory* in the sense that there is a definite relation between tension, systems, disruptions, and properties of the environment.

Lewin (1946) referenced socially induced change, arguing that tension and valences may be aroused socially. Forces acting on a person may arise from an individual's own needs or be imposed. For example, if people are not motivated to work, or lack any intrinsic interest in their jobs, they may be inclined to waste time. However, the presence of a supervisor will induce forces in the direction of performing work. When this supervising force is not present, workers can get back to wasting time.

Although mobile phones may be ideally suited for the delivery of persuasive messages—messages that will motivate an individual to change—individuals must first be receptive to the message before they will make any changes to their attitude or behavior. Several theorists (Deci and Ryan, 1985; Fishbein and Ajzen, 1975) maintain that there is only a single type of intrinsic motivation, which can be described as a motivation to engage in activities that enhance or maintain a person's self-concept. Other theorists (Lepper and Malone, 1987) posit that there are several factors that will influence motivation. Intrinsic motivators, as examined in Lepper and Malone's classic analysis, are innate motivational factors that can be leveraged through good design to bring about behavior change. The authors identify numerous factors that contribute to intrinsic motivation, of which five are particularly relevant to mobile computing research. These motivators are frequently referenced as factors contributing to successful behavior change—in this case, using a device—and they include challenge (the setting of goals that are adequately difficult, but not impossible to reach), control (the individual's perceived ability to exert control over their environment or an application), competition (comparing oneself to others with a desire to outperform), cooperation (working with others toward a common goal), and recognition (positive feedback in direct response to an accomplishment).

4.2.4   Feedback

A final motivational and persuasive factor that can be provided with computers is concept of *feedback*. In general, feedback can be presented in one of two ways: positive or negative. Research has typically shown that positive feedback is a stronger mechanism for affecting long-term adaptation of new behavior than negative feedback. Ilies and Judge (2005) have shown that when given feedback across time, individuals constantly adjusted their goals to close the goal-outcome gap. Positive feedback indicating goal attainment led individuals to set higher subsequent goals, and negative feedback indicating goal nonattainment led them to adjust subsequent goals downward. As a result, individuals repeatedly strived to improve their performance, regardless of whether they achieved their goals. Feedback can encourage people to strive for better performance.

Experimental work on the level of aspiration in individuals has indicated that cultural and group factors tend to establish reference points that help determine the level of difficulty of goals set by individuals. For example, in most weight loss groups in Western cultures, and under pressure for self-improvement, most people will indicate a level (of aspiration) above their previous level of attainment. In addition, an individual's level of aspiration is likely to be very much influenced by the standards of the group to which he or she belongs (Festinger, 1954; Wood, 2003).

For example, Lin et al. (2006) have demonstrated that feedback works for individuals interacting with a virtual pet in their work with the pedometer-based game Fish'n'Steps. In Fish'n'Steps, the user is given a virtual fish that resides on their computer whose state is determined by the number of steps the user takes on a daily basis, as recorded by a simple pedometer. The fish increasing in size is positive feedback and the fish decreasing in size is negative feedback. Lin et al. did not directly examine the nature of feedback experimentally, but their findings still showed that a number of subjects who received negative feedback stopped playing the game altogether ostensibly to avoid the negative interactions with their fish.

Consolvo et al. (2008) have developed a design schema for providing feedback to a user based on his or her physical activity as measured by an accelerometer and various activity sensing algorithms. In their design, users were given only positive feedback. Feedback was presented to the user in the form of an ever-changing image of a garden, displayed on the mobile phone desktop. In the application, called Ubifit Garden, a user's physical actions are translated into new additions to the desktop image, such as flowers, plants, and butterflies, depending on the types and amount of activity conducted by the user. The design of the application is well grounded in the theories of persuasion, but empirical data to validate the concept are still forthcoming. In the next section, I will describe how we applied intrinsic motivators including competition, cooperation, control, and feedback recognition to a mobile health game application. These factors have been shown to bring about behavior change in many circumstances.

4.3   A MOBILE HEALTH GAME: USING SOCIAL INFLUENCE TO CHANGE BEHAVIOR

Childhood obesity is a national epidemic. Since the 1990s, childhood and adolescent obesity has sky rocketed [Center for Disease Control and Prevention (CDC) Report, 2008]. Not only is obesity a health risk, but being overweight during adolescence is related to declines in physical, social, emotional, and academic development. In fact, during the past 20 years there has been a dramatic increase in obesity in the entire population in the United States. In 2007, only one state (Colorado) had a prevalence of obesity less than 20%. Thirty states had a prevalence equal to or greater than 25% (CDC Report, 2008).

Social influence has been shown to play an important role in persuasion and the motivation of behavior change; countless studies, both involving technology and not, have shown that individuals grouped with peers have better results in quitting drinking, quitting smoking, losing weight, exercising, and even surviving cancer (Fogg and Eckles, 2007).

Computer-based social support, particularly over the Internet, poses an interesting alternative or supplement to more traditional forms of social support. Preece (1999a) has extensively explored social interactions in online communities and has in fact found that social support, much of in the form of empathy among members, is present in most communities. In work more specifically targeted toward social support, Preece (1999b) finds that individuals congregate in medically focused online communities to seek out both facts and empathy from individuals facing similar circumstances. Although this work demonstrated that fact-finding was suboptimal in most cases, empathy and social support were readily available to members and were, in many cases, the driving force in such interactions.

Furthermore, online discussion forums have been shown to benefit cancer patients while offering broader accessibility and a higher degree of privacy (Fernsler and Manchester, 1997). Unlike scheduled weekly meetings or even friends who may not be readily available to speak by phone or in person, online forums are ever-present, and because of time differences and the infinite geography of the World Wide Web, are active at nearly any time of day (Wallace, 1999). Wallace (1999) and McKenna et al. (2007) have shown that relationship and group formation is often significantly improved via computer-mediated communication such as message boards as described above, and Joinson (2001) has shown that self-disclosure is easier and occurs more frequently than in face-to-face encounters. As such, not only does this technology provide patients with greater access to their peer support group, but in theory, they should be able to form strong bonds with one another and feel comfortable sharing personal information and thought.

Gump and Kulik (1997) present further evidence that individuals facing stressful situations are more likely to affiliate with one another. In particular, their findings demonstrated that individuals who believed they were facing a similar stressful situation (i.e., the same source of stress) were more likely to affiliate with one another than those facing different sources of stress. As such, even groups of users who start out as relative strangers may soon begin to form closer relationships.

The Mindless Eating Challenge (MEC) is aimed at addressing obesity through the use of mobile technology and virtual support groups. The MEC is a mobile phone-based application, or game, geared toward children. In essence, the game is centered on accountability, and asks that the user becomes responsible for the well-being of a virtual character by eating healthily (Gay et al., 2008). MEC aims to encourage healthy behavior through emotional support, feedback, and social connectivity (Yuan and Gay, 2006). Features of the application include Global Positioning System, high-quality cameras, and the ability to use one's own mobile phone as the primary device for many different functions (email, scheduling, storing contacts, way-finding, etc.). Furthermore, the technology behind MEC provides developers with many new means of interacting with and delivering messages to the user to encourage them to change attitudes and behavior (Fogg, 2002). The MEC thus uses various forms of motivation—both social and individual—to encourage healthy behavior. The designers developed a system that could be used to encourage a richer interaction between users and public spaces, and are particularly interested in applications of social facilitation and influence (Zajonc, 1965; Cialdini, 2001).

Adolescents use the mobile phone for much more than making phone calls. They increasingly view their phones as an immediate and entertaining link to their entire social network and, in turn, as an essential partner in the construction and organization of their social identity. Between the ages of 11 and 15 years, cell phone ownership jumps to 37%, and by the time teens are 17 years old, nearly 60% own a phone. These numbers are growing (Lenhart et al., 2005). However, this is no surprise, because these media-savvy teens still have one thing in common with teens of pervious generations: they rely less on their parents and more on their peers during this developmental transition into adulthood. Teens today are driving the use of new mobile technologies built into their phones. Services such as text messaging, camera phones, and multimedia messaging systems (MMS) are used by more than half of teens with mobile phones (Ernest-Jones, 2004). The mobile phone can provide an instrument with which teens textually and visually connect to each other, remain entertained, while simultaneously constructing their own identities.

Typically, people of all ages view their personal phones as being highly supportive of their social life and activities. MEC seeks to examine how this type of social interaction, when coupled with interaction (and the resulting accountability) with virtual pets, can be used to help young people maintain healthy eating and exercise routines (Gay et al., 2008; Cialdini, 2006). The goal is founded upon the notion that computer games have the potential to motivate learners and can be used as effective tools for behavior change (Lepper and Malone, 1987). It then follows that the combination of mobile phones and games could be an extremely potent tool for helping individuals achieve and maintain better personal health, especially since so much health-related behavior, from eating to exercise, takes place while people are on the go.

In MEC, the player will be tasked with caring for a virtual pet, plant, or other character that resides on their mobile phone. Past incarnations of virtual pets, particularly the well-known Tamagotchi, have demonstrated that such a simple game can captivate a massive and broad audience. In MEC, the player first selects a character from a variety of choices, including cartoon renditions of various standard household pets, plants, creatures, or other abstract characters (Gay et al., 2008). The chosen character will then reside on the player's mobile phone and interact with the player through a series of prompts and messages throughout the day (Figure 4.2). The catch, however, is that the requests made by the character are derived from tips for better eating developed at the Cornell University Food and Brand Laboratory (Wansink, 2006). Furthermore, the player only gets credit for fulfilling the request by taking a photo, with their phone's built-in camera, of themselves carrying out the task. For example, a virtual pet could ask for a "hot breakfast this morning, such as oatmeal," and the player would have to take a picture him or herself eating a bowl of oatmeal (Figure

FIGURE 4.2: The character responds to the player's actions by adding or removing features, accessories, etc. (Gay et al., 2008).

4.3). The pet then provides feedback via a thank you message and by slightly modifying its appearance; it can do such things as modify its expression, its physique, its apparent energy level, or gain accessories. In addition to these changes in the pet's appearance, players are given scores based on their compliance to requests from the pet. Players are also required to provide their daily weight to the game. In a social component to the game, players are able to log into a web site and track their performance, see other players' photos, converse with others, share their pets with one another, and judge one another's photos (Figure 4.4).

The purpose of our mobile phone game is to reward good health habits and food choices. The application uses theories of persuasion in a game that promotes healthy behaviors in daily life.

From a human–computer interaction perspective, the aim of the MEC research is to understand how mobile phones can be used to employ various forms of motivation—both social and individual—to encourage healthy behavior. Intrinsic motivators supplied by the system include are innate motivational factors such as competition, cooperation, control, and recognition that have been leveraged to bring about behavior change in many circumstances (Gay et al., 2008).

FIGURE 4.3: A young person demonstrates compliance by taking a picture and submitting it for review.

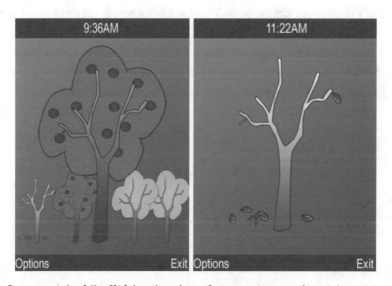

FIGURE 4.4: Leaves might fall off if the player's performance is poor. A social portion of the game allows the user to see various depictions of their performance in comparison to the performance of others in their group, as well as of their group in comparison to other groups.

In addition to feedback received from the system or from peers via the mobile phone, and through repeated long-term use, individuals will require some real-world feedback or evidence that their new learned behavior is in fact having a positive net outcome. The feedback given is derived from a well-researched and validated system of recommendations and tips for healthier eating developed at the Cornell University Food and Brand Laboratory. The central theme of the research, and the derived tips that are made available to users, center on the premise that understanding environmental influences on food consumption behavior has immediate implications for consumer welfare (Cutler et al., 2003). People, for example, do not often accurately monitor their basic level of consumption and can often underestimate actual intake, which can lead to overeating and eventually obesity (Wansink et al., 1998). Use of these tips provides users with simple and validated persuasive messages that can be used as the source for the mobile health game.

4.4   CONCLUSION

Although the overarching goal of MEC is to teach and instill better eating habits in an adolescent population, the benefits of the game as a tool for research are invaluable. The study of persuasive technology in the mobile context is certainly well grounded in existing theory and impressive work has been done to date to examine some of the relevant theoretical constructs (Fogg, 2002). One of the most powerful features of location-based media is its ability to persuade or coach in context.

In particular, mobile technologies can encourage social facilitation—the notion that individuals are more likely to perform simple or well-learned behaviors if they believe that their behavior is being observed; social comparison, which posits that individuals seek to perform at a similar level to those around them; and social cognition, which among other things asserts that individuals tend to model their behavior around those around them, particularly those who appear to be successful. Through good design, all of these motivational factors can be used and studied in mobile phone applications (Cialdini, 2006).

CHAPTER 5

Ethical Issues and Final Thoughts

As we discussed in the first section of this monograph, the integration of mobile resources into physical spaces can potentially affect the development, maintenance, and transformation of communities and social interactions, and relations with context. Ubiquitous mobile computing allows users to engage in activities in diverse physical locations, to access resources specific to the location, and to communicate directly or indirectly with others. Mobile technologies can potentially enhance social interactions and users' experiences. However, as I had attempted to point out, activities using mobile devices in context generate complex systems of interactions, and the benefits of ubiquity and mobility can easily be lost if that complexity is not appreciated and understood.

In both activity theory and social constructivist approaches, shared objectives and collective task orientation are critical constituent features of productive interactions (Kuutti, 1995; Wenger, 1998). The current emphasis on hybrid spaces, however, focuses on the impact of digital technologies' relatively new movement away from the desktop setting and formulaic goal-oriented tasks. Spaces, the objects within them, and the events transpiring there, all encourage and afford certain behaviors (Gibson, 1979). The design of the space should suggest the type of activity or interaction associated with the space. People orient to these affordances and tend to adapt practices from the physical world to the affordances of electronic space. To facilitate this transfer, virtual communities must be visible from the outside and provide cues for activities once people join a community (Dieberger, 1999).

Whereas designers used to look predominantly toward spatial metaphors and lessons from the design of physical environments to help organize desktop interfaces, we now look to how digital interfaces become part of the configuration of everyday places. Therefore, there is the need to look at tools in relation to one another, that is, to the relationship between face-to-face communication and mediated communication spaces and to the relationship between the simultaneous interactions in mediated and physical spaces available through mobile communication devices.

5.1 ETHICS AND MOBILE TECHNOLOGIES

New technologies provide opportunities for the collection of new types of information. For example, computer-based tracking applications can reveal users' locations, friends and associates, time of interactions, data accessed, notes, etc. These tools can disclose behaviors and social phenomena that have remained hidden and unexamined, even unimagined, because the technologies required to reveal them did not exist until recently. Because new technologies enable new ways of knowing, and new ways of representing and reporting activity, they pose methodological, social, and ethical challenges upon which the people who design and control these applications need to reflect and which they should proactively address.

Mobile tracking devices can be used as an unobtrusive means of collecting data to, for example, evaluate the efficiency or usability of mobile applications and the use of a device in a particular location. On the positive side, such tools can contribute to richly descriptive feedback for system designers, for example, assessing whether and how a mobile health program influenced a particular group to exercise or how a user navigates physical and online spaces in order to find information or locate people interested in a similar topic.

However, such unobtrusive, but potentially invasive, technologies raise numerous concerns regarding surveillance, dataveillance, confidentiality, privacy, anonymity, and informed consent. Furthermore, they potentially threaten multiple trust relationships, for example, when tracking devices are used to monitor employee performance or productivity. Even monitoring how users navigate a site or use information resources (e.g., a library catalog) while maintaining anonymity can violate users' expectations of privacy and anonymity when they are unaware that their actions are being recorded. In fact, tracking tools raise serious legal and ethical questions about the nature of privacy and even the distinction between public and private, as do many emerging technologies.

Activity theory cautions us that the use of any tool potentially transforms the activity in which it is used, and, reciprocally, tools are transformed in the process of their use. New context-aware tools and interactive technologies enable as well as mediate new ways of knowing and new ways of experiencing the world. However, any technology simultaneously conceals, reveals, and directs attention and actions in particular ways. Responsible human–computer interaction (HCI) professionals need to reflect on that potential, along with other ethical considerations in the mediating functions of technologies both in the design and delivery of applications using such tools especially with vulnerable populations. There is a need for HCI professionals to document and critically analyze situated uses of mobile technology in various settings and in design activities themselves to fully understand the mediating functions and potential of different technologies and tools.

5.1.1   Creating a Sense of Place

We can return now to the key questions outlined in the Introduction. First, how does people's existing sense of place influence their appropriation of technology for new activities? The activities we are seeking to support in the implementation described here are reflections on presence, in the form of people's patterns and preferences, and personal acts of creative expression. How might these new activities be supported by mobile technology in various contexts? Research in social navigation often deals with real-world concepts of social navigation (e.g., getting directions or recommending a book) and applying these concepts to online information spaces. We are interested in how technologies and people can become more aware of both physical and social contexts. How does the device track activity and interpret contextual information and what should it tell you once data are collected? How do technologies, people, and physical environments shape behavior and experiences? How do HCI designers make sure that the information is not competing with the object, that users do not become distracted or overloaded, and how do users gain control over the tools and information in their lives?

Designing context-aware technology also highlights the importance of the actual physical space—and the unique experiences, through opportunities and restrictions, that this physicality creates. After years of heralding the anytime, anyplace nature of technology, we can now return to exploring the sacredness of a particular time and a particular space.

The built environment has always existed as a hybrid space with multiple technologies contributing to the sensing, manipulating, and understanding of the world in general and everyday experiences in particular. The current emphasis on hybrid spaces, however, focuses on the impact of digital technologies' relatively new movement away from the desktop setting and formulaic goal-oriented tasks. Whereas designers used to look predominantly toward spatial metaphors and lessons from the design of physical environments to help organize desktop interfaces, we now look to how digital interfaces become part of the configuration of everyday places.

Context-aware technologies in museums, for example, have been of two general varieties. One follows the traditional trajectory of using technology to deliver content in context. The second approach to context-aware computing follows the traditional agenda for context-aware computing in general, that is, making systems aware of the user's context. Location-aware systems, for example, track the user's location in order to serve the right information at the right time. Another application of location awareness combined with profile building uses a visitor's usage pattern information to deduce what information is most interesting to the visitor and changing the experience accordingly (Munro et al., 1999). These devices can also be used to help people connect with others and the world around them (Sengers et al., 2008). Leveraging social connections to support meaningful experience is a promising approach for designers to explore. On the Web, interaction has evolved from one-way information push to interactive information seeking to explicit social interaction. We expect a similar trend in other computing contexts. Tools and services for sharing, recording, and distributing social information in physical contexts will become more common. Users will partner with computing devices to gather and interpret contextual information. When this happens, we expect that people's expectations of what computers do in the wild will move from informational goals toward social ones.

.   .   .   .   .

Bibliography

Abowd, G., Atkeson, C., Hong, J., Long, S., Kooper, R., and Pinkerton, M. (1997). Cyberguide: A mobile context-aware tour guide. *Wireless Networks*, 3(5), pp. 421–433.

Agre, P. (1997). *Computation and human experience*. Cambridge, UK: Cambridge University Press.

Ahern, S., Davis, M., Eckles, D., King, S., Naaman, M., Nair, R., Spasojevic, M., Hui, I., and Yang, J. (2006). Zonetag: Designing context-aware mobile media capture to increase participation. PICS'06, 3, Orange County, CA.

Alexander, C., Ishikawa, S., Silverstein, M., Jacobson, M., Fiksdahl-King, I., and Angel, S. (1977). *A Pattern Language*. New York, NY: Oxford University Press.

Ames, M., and Naaman, M. (2007). Why we tag: Motivations for annotation in mobile and online media. In *Proceedings of CHI'07*, pp. 971–980, San Jose, CA.

Ark, W., Dryer, D., and Lu, D. (1999). The emotion mouse. In *Proceedings of HCI'99*, pp. 818–823, Munich, Germany.

Bandura, A. (1986). *Social Foundations of Thought and Action: A Social Cognitive Theory*. Englewood Cliffs, NJ: Prentice-Hall.

Bandura, A. (1997). *Self-Efficacy: The Exercise of Control*. New York, NY: Freeman.

Bandura, A., and Walters, R. (1963). *Social Learning and Personality Development*. New York, NY: Holt, Rinehart and Winston.

Barkhuus, L., Brown, B., Bell, M., Sherwood, S., Hall, M., and Chalmers, M. (2008). From awareness to repartee: Sharing location within social groups. In *Proceedings of SIGCHI'08*, pp. 497–506, Florence, Italy. doi:10.1145/1357054.1357134

Bell, G. (2002). Making sense of the museum: The museum as 'cultural ecology': A study. CIMI whitepaper, Intel Corporation.

Boehner, K., Gay, G., and Hembrooke, H. (2005a). Designing for a sense of place: Imprints of presence. In *Proceedings of CHCI'05*, Las Vegas, NV.

Boehner, K., Gay, G., and Larkin, C. (2005b). Drawing evaluation into design for mobile computing: A case study of the Renwick Gallery's handheld education project. *International Journal
of Digital Libraries*, 5(3), pp. 219–230. doi:10.1007/s00799-004-0107-7

Boehner, K., Sengers, P., and Gay, G. (2005c). Affective presence in museums: Ambient systems
for creative expression. *Journal of Digital Creativity*, 16(2), pp. 79–89. doi:10.1080/NDCR-
117286

Boehner, K., Sengers, P., Medynskiy, Y., and Gay, G. (2005d). Opening the frame of the art museum: Technology as art and tool. In *Proceedings of DACC'05*, pp. 123–132, Copenhagen,
Denmark.

Boehner, K., Thom-Santelli, J., Zoss, A., Gay, G., Barrett, T., and Hall, J. (2005e). Imprints of place:
Creative expressions of the museum experience. In *Proceedings of CHI'05*, pp. 1220–1223,
Portland, OR. doi:10.1145/1056808.1056881

Broadbent, J., and Marti, P. (1997). Location-aware mobile interactive guides: Usability issues. In
Proceedings of ICHIM'97, pp. 25–35, Paris, France.

Brown, B., MacColl, I., Chalmers, M., Galani, A., Randell, C., and Steed, A. (2003). Lessons from
the lighthouse: Collaboration in a shared mixed reality system. In *Proceedings of CHI'03*,
pp. 577–584, Ft. Lauderdale, FL. doi:10.1145/642611.642711

Brown, B., and Perry, M. (2002). Of maps and guidebooks: Designing geographical technologies.
In *Proceedings of DIS'02*, pp. 246–254, Osaka, Japan.

Burrell, J., and Gay, G. (2001). Collectively defining context in a mobile, networked computing
environment. In *Proceedings of CHIC'01*, Seattle, WA. doi:10.1145/634067.634205

Burrell, J., and Gay, G. (2002). E-graffiti: Evaluating real-world use of a context-aware system. *Interacting with Computers*, 14(4), pp. 301–312. doi:10.1016/S0953-5438(02)00010-3

Burrell, J., Gay, G., Kubo, K., and Farina, N. (2002). Context-aware computing: A test case. In
Borriello, G., and Holmquist, L. (Eds.), *Proceedings of UBICOMP'02* (pp. 1–15), Goteborg,
Sweden. doi:10.1007/3-540-45809-3_1

Canter, D. (1977). *The Psychology of Place*. London, UK: Architectural Press Ltd.

Castrenze, P. (2008). Traces of place: An audio documentary and essay. Thesis, Cornell University
Center for Disease Control and Prevention (2008). *Overweight and Obesity*. Washington,
DC: Department of Health and Human Services. Retrieved from http://www.cdc.gov/
nccdphp/dnpa/obesity/.

Cheverst, K., Davies, N., Mitchell, K., Friday, A., and Efstratiou, C. (2000). Developing a context-
aware electronic tourist guide: Some issues and experiences. In *Proceedings of CHI'00*, The
Hague, Netherlands.

Cialdini, R. (2001). *Influence: Science and Practice (4th edition)*, Boston, MA: Allyn and Bacon.

Cialdini, R. (2006). *Influence: The Psychology of Persuasion*. Collins Business Essentials (Eds.), New York, NY: William Morrow.

Ciavarella, C., and Paternò, F. (2004). The design of a handheld, location-aware guide for indoor environments. *Personal and Ubiquitous Computing*, 8(2), pp. 82–91. doi:10.1007/s00779-004-0265-z

Ciolfi, L., and Bannon, L. (2003). Learning from museum visits: Shaping design sensitivities. In *Proceedings in HCII'03*, Pittsburgh, PA.

Clark, H. (1996). *Using Language*. Cambridge, MA: Cambridge University Press.

Clark, H., and Brennan, S. (1991). Grounding in communication. In Levine, J., Resnick, L., and Behrend, S. (Eds.), *Shared Cognition: Thinking as Social Practice*. Washington, DC: APA. doi:10.1037/10096-006

Clark, H., and Wilkes-Gibbes, D. (1986). Referring as a collaborative process. *Cognition*, 22, pp. 1–39. doi:10.1016/0010-0277(86)90010-7

Consolvo, S., Froehlich, J., Harrison, B., Klansnja, P., LaMarca, A., LeGrand, L., Smith, I., Toscos, T., McDonald, D., and Landay, J. (2008). Activity sensing in the wild: A field trial of UbiFit Garden. In *Proceedings of CHI'08*, Florence, Italy. doi:10.1145/1357054.1357335

Cooper, A. (1999). *The Inmates Are Running the Asylum*. Indianapolis, IN: Sams.

Cosley, D., Baxter, J., Lee, S., Alson, B., Adams, P., Sarabu, C., Nomura, S., and Gay, G. (2009). A tag in the hand: Supporting semantic, social, and spatial navigation in museums. In *Proceedings of CHI'09*, Boston, MA.

Cosley, D., Frankowski, D., Kiesler, S., Terveen, L., and Riedl, J. (2005). How oversight improves member-maintained communities. In *Proceedings of CHI'05*, pp. 11–20, Portland, OR. doi:10.1145/1054972.1054975

Cosley, D., Lewenstein, J., Herman, A., Holloway, J., Baxter, J., Nomura, S., Boehner, K., and Gay, G. (2008). ArtLinks: Fostering social awareness and reflection in museums. In *Proceedings of CHI'08*, pp. 403–412, Florence, Italy.

Cresswell, T. (2004). *Place: A Short Introduction*. Malden, MA: Blackwell.

Cutler, D., Glaeser, E., and Shapiro, J. (2003). Why have Americans become more obese? *Journal of Economic Perspectives*, 17(3), pp. 93–118. doi:10.1257/089533003769204371

Daft, R., and Lengle, R. (1984). Information richness: A new approach to managerial behavior and organizational design. *Research in Organizational Behavior*, 6, pp. 191–233.

Deci, E., and Ryan, M. (1985). *Intrinsic Motivation and Self-Determination in Human Behavior*. New York, NY: Plenum.

Dey, A. (2001). Understanding and using context. *Personal Ubiquitous Computing*, 5(1), pp. 4–7. doi:10.1007/s007790170019

Dey, A., and Abowd, G. (2000). Towards a better understanding of context and context-awareness. In *Proceedings of CHI'00*, The Hague, Netherlands.

Dey, A., Abowd, G., and Salber, D. (2001). A conceptual framework and toolkit for supporting the rapid prototyping of context-aware applications. *Journal of Human-Computer Interaction*, 16(2), pp. 97–166. doi:10.1207/S15327051HCI16234_02

Dieberger, A. (1999). Social connotations of space in the design for virtual communities and social navigation. In Munro, A., Hook, K., and Benyon, D. (Eds.), *Social Navigation of Information Space*. Berlin: Springer-Verlag.

DiMicco, J., Pandolfo, A., and Bender, W. (2004). Influencing group participation with a shared display. In *Proceedings of CSCW'04*, pp. 614–623, Chicago, IL. doi:10.1145/1031607.1031713

Dourish, P. (1999). Where the footprints lead: Tracking down other roles for social navigation. In Munro, A., Hook, K., and Benyon, D. (Eds.), *Social Navigation of Information Space*. New York, NY: Springer-Verlag.

Dourish, P. (2006). Re-space-ing place: "Place" and "space" ten years on. In *Proceedings of CSCW'06*, pp. 299–308, Banff, Alberta, Canada. doi:10.1145/1180875.1180921

Dourish, P., and Chalmers, M. (1994). Running out of space: Models of information navigation. In *Proceedings of HCI'94*, Glasgow, Scotland.

Eckles, D. (2007). Redefining persuasion for a mobile world. In Fogg, B., and Eckles, D. (Eds.), *Mobile Persuasion: 20 Perspectives on the Future of Behavioral Change* (pp. 143–149). Stanford, CA: Stanford Captology Media.

Engestrom, Y., Miettinen, R., and Punamaki, R. (Eds.) (1999). *Perspectives on Activity Theory (Learning in Doing Social, Cognitive and Computations Perspectives)*. Cambridge, UK: Cambridge University Press.

Erickson, T., and Kellogg, W. (2001). Social translucence: An approach to designing systems that support social processes. *ACM Transactions on Computer-Human Interaction*, 7(1), pp. 59–83.

Erickson, T., Kellogg, W., Smith, D., Laff, M., Richards, J., and Bradner, E. (1999). Socially translucent systems: Social proxies, persistent conversation, and the design of "babble." *In Proceedings of CHI'99*, pp. 72–79, Pittsburgh, PA. doi:10.1145/302979.302997

Ernest-Jones, T. (2004). White Paper—*MMS Evolution*. Hampshire, England: Juniper Research Limited.

Espinoza, F., Persson, P., Sandin, A., Nyström, H., Cacciatore, E., and Bylund, M. (2001). GeoNotes: Social and navigational aspects of location-based information systems. In *Proceedings of UBICOMP'01*, pp. 2–17, Atlanta, GA. doi:10.1007/3-540-45427-6_2

Falk, H., and Dierking, L. (1992). *The Museum Experience*. Washington, DC: Whalesback Books.

Feiner, S. (2002). Augmented reality: A new way of seeing. *Scientific American*, 286(4), pp. 34–41.

Fernandez, R., Scheirer, J., and Picard, R. (1999). Expression glasses: A wearable device for facial expression recognition. In *Proceedings of CHI'99*, p. 484, Pittsburgh, PA.

Fernsler, J., and Manchester, L. (1997). Evaluation of a computer-based cancer support network. *Cancer Practice*, 5(1), pp. 46–51.

Ferris, K., Bannon, L., Ciolfi, L., Gallagher, P., Hall, T., and Lennon, M. (2004). Shaping experiences in the Hunt Museum: A design case study. In *Proceedings of DIS'04*, pp. 205–214, Cambridge, MA. doi:10.1145/1013115.1013144

Festinger, L. (1954). A theory of social comparison processes. *Human Relations*, 7, pp. 114–140. doi:10.1177/001872675400700202

Festinger, L. (1957). *A Theory of Cognitive Dissonance*. Stanford, CA: Stanford University Press.

Finlay, I. (1977). *Priceless Heritage: The Future of Museums*. London, UK: Faber and Faber.

Finn, K., Sellen, A., and Wilbur, S. (1977). *Video-Mediated Communication*. Hillsdale, NJ: Erlbaum.

Fishbein, M., and Ajzen, I. (1975). *Belief, Attitude, Intention, and Behavior: An Introduction to Theory and Research*. Reading, MA: Addison-Wesley.

Fleck, M., Frid, M., Kindberg, T., O'Brien-Strain, E., Rajani, R., and Spasojevic, M. (2002). From informing to remembering: Ubiquitous systems in interactive museums. *Pervasive Computing*, 1(2), pp. 13–21. doi:10.1109/MPRV.2002.1012333

Fogg, B. (2002). *Persuasive Technology. Using Computers to Change What We Think and Do*. San Francisco, CA: Morgan Kaufmann.

Fogg, B., and Eckles, D. (2007). *Mobile Persuasion: 20 Perspectives on the Future of Behavioral Change*, pp. 143–149, Stanford, CA: Stanford Captology Media.

Fulk, J., Schmitz, J., and Ryu, D. (1995). Cognitive elements in the social construction of communication technology. *Management Communication Quarterly*, 8(3), pp. 259–288. doi:10.1177/0893318995008003001

Galani, A., and Chalmers, M. (2004). Production of place as a collaborative activity. In *Proceedings of CHI'04*, pp. 1417–1420, New York, NY.

Gavers, W. (1992). The affordances of media spaces for collaboration. In *Proceedings of CSCW'92*, Toronto Ontario, Canada.

Gay, G., Boehner, K., and Panella, T. (1997). ArtView: Transforming image databases into collaborative learning spaces. *Journal of Educational Computing Research*, 16(4), pp. 317–332. doi:10.2190/J8VK-WNVQ-Q03R-H56A

Gay, G., Byrne, S., and Pollak, J. (2008). Mindless eating challenge. Report to the Robert Wood Johnson Foundation Pioneer Grants Program.

Gay, G., and Hembrooke, H. (2002). Browsing behaviors in wireless learning networks. In *Proceedings of HICSS'02*, Big Island, HI.

Gay, G., and Hembrooke, H. (2004). *Activity Centered Design*. Cambridge, MA: MIT Press.

Gay, G., Pollak, J., and Leonard, J. (2009). Mobile health: Social influence and emotional support in context. Proposal, NIH.

Gersie, A., Benyon, D., Munro, A., and Höök, K. (Eds.) (2003). *Designing Information Spaces: The Social Navigation Approach*. London, UK: Springer-Verlag.

Gibson, J. (1979). *The Ecological Approach to Visual Perception*. Boston, MA: Houghton Mifflin.

Giddens, A. (1979). *Central Problems in Social Theory: Action, Structure and Contradiction in Social Analysis*. London, UK: Macmillan.

Goffman, E. (1971). *Relations in Public: Microstudies of the Public Order*. New York, NY: Basic Books.

Greenberg, S. (2001). Context as a dynamic construct. *Journal of Human-Computer Interaction*, 16(2), pp. 257–268. doi:10.1207/S15327051HCI16234_09

Grinter, R., Aoki, P., Hurst, A., Szymanski, M., Thornton, J., and Woodruff, A. (2002). Revisiting the visit: Understanding how technology can shape the museum visit. In *Proceedings of CSCW'02*, pp. 146–155, New Orleans, LA. doi:10.1145/587078.587100

Grudin, J. (1990). Why CSCW applications fail: Problems in the design and evaluation of organizational interfaces. In *Proceedings of CSCW'90*, pp. 85–93, Portland, OR.

Gump, B., and Kulik, J. (1997). Stress, affiliation, and emotional contagion. *Journal of Personality and Social Psychology*, 72(2), pp. 305–319. doi:10.1037/0022-3514.72.2.305

Halkia, M., and Local, G. (2003). Building the brief: Action and audience in augmented reality. In *Proceedings of HCII'03*, Pittsburgh, PA.

Harrison, S., and Dourish, P. (1996). *Re-placing Space: The Roles of Place and Space in Collaborative Systems*. In *Proceedings of CSCW'96*, pp. 67–76, Boston, MA.

Heath, C., Luff, P., vom Lehn, D., and Hindmarsh, J. (2002). Crafting participation: Designing ecologies, configuring experience. *Visual Communication*, 1(1), pp. 9–33. doi:10.1177/147035720200100102

Hillier, B. (1996). *Space Is the Machine*. Cambridge, MA: Cambridge University Press.

Hillier B., Hanson, J., and Peponis, J. (1984). What do we mean by building function? In Powell, J., Cooper, I., and Lera, S. (Eds.), *Designing for Building Utilization*. London, UK: Spon.

Hook, K., Benyon, D., and Munro, A. (2003). *Designing Information Spaces: The Social Navigation Approach*. Berlin: Springer-Verlag.

Hornecker, E., and Stifter, M. (2006). Learning from interactive museum installations: About interaction design for public settings. In *Proceedings of OZCHI'06*, pp. 135–142, Sydney, Australia. doi:10.1145/1228175.1228201

Hovland, C., Janis, I., and Kelley, H. (1953). *Communication and Persuasion: Psychological Studies of Opinion Change*. New Haven, CT: Yale University Press.

Hovland, C., Lumsdaine, A., and Sheffield, F. (1949). *Experiments on Mass Communication. Studies in Social Psychology in World War II* (Vol. 3). Princeton, NJ: Princeton University Press.

Hubbard, P., Kitchin, R., and Valentine, G. (Eds). (2004). *Key Thinkers on Space and Place*. London, UK: Sage Publications.

Iishi, K. (2006). Implications of mobility: The uses of personal communication media in everyday life. *Journal of Communication*, 56(2), pp. 346–365. doi:10.1111/j.1460-2466.2006.00023.x

Ilies, R., and Judge, T. (2005). Goal regulation across time: The effects of feedback and affect. *Journal of Applied Psychology*, 90(3), pp. 453–467. doi:10.1037/0021-9010.90.3.453

Janssen, J., Erkens, G., Kanselaar, G., and Jaspers, J. (2007). Visualization of participation: Does it contribute to successful computer-supported collaborative learning? *Computers and Education*, 49, pp. 1037–1065. doi:10.1016/j.compedu.2006.01.004

Joinson, A. (2001). Self-disclosure in computer-mediated communication: The role of self-awareness and visual anonymity. *European Journal of Social Psychology*, 31(2), pp. 177–192. doi:10.1002/ejsp.36

Joseph, A., de Lespinasse, A., Tauber, J., Gifford, D., and Kaashoek, M. (1995). Rover: A toolkit for mobile information access. In *Proceedings of SOSP'95*, pp. 156–171, Cooper Mountain Resort, CO.

Jung, C. (1964). *Man and His Symbols*. New York, NY: Bantam Doubleday Dell.

Karau, S., and Williams, K. (2001). Understanding individual motivation in groups: The collective effort model. In Turner, M. (Ed.), *Groups at Work: Theory and Research*. Mahwah, NJ: Erlbaum.

Kulyk, O., Wang, J., and Terken, J. (2006). Real-time feedback on nonverbal behavior to enhance social dynamics in small group meetings. In *Proceedings of MLMI'05*, pp. 150–161, Edinburgh, UK. doi:10.1007/11677482_13

Kuutti, K. (1995). Activity theory as a potential framework for human–computer interaction research. In B. Nardi (Ed.), *Context and Consciousness: Activity Theory and Human Computer Interaction*. Cambridge: MIT Press.

vom Lehn, D., Hindmarsh, J., Luff, P., and Heath, C. (2007). Engaging constable: Revealing art with new technology. In *Proceedings of CHI'07*, pp. 1485–1494, San José, CA.

Lenhart A., Madden, M., and Hitlin, P. (2005). *Teens and Technology: Youth Are Leading the Transition to a Fully Wired and Mobile Nation*. Washington, DC: Pew Internet and American Life Project.

Leont'ev, A. (1981). *Problems of the Development of Mind*. English translation, Moscow: Progress Press (Russian original 1947).

Lepper, M., and Malone, T. (1987). Intrinsic motivation and instructional effectiveness in computer-based education. In Snow, R., and Farr, M. (Eds.), *Aptitude, Learning and Instruction: III. Cognitive and Affective Process Analyses* (pp. 255–286). Hillsdale, NJ: Erlbaum.

Leshed, G., Hancock, J., Cosley, D., McLeod, P., and Gay, G. (2007). Feedback for guiding reflection on teamwork practices. In *Proceedings of GROUP'07*, Sanibel Island, FL. doi:10.1145/1316624.1316655

Lewin, K. (1938). *The Conceptual Representation and the Measurement of Psychological Forces*. Durham, NC: Duke University Press.

Lewin, K. (1946). Action research and minority problems. *Journal of Social Issues*, 2(4), pp. 4–34.

Lin, J., Mamykina, L., Lindtner, S., Delajoux, G., and Strub, H. (2006). Fish'n'Steps: Encouraging physical activity with an interactive computer game. In *Proceedings of Ubicomp'06*, Orange County, CA. doi:10.1007/11853565_16

Lombard, M., and Ditton, T. (1997). At the heart of it all: The concept of presence. *Journal of Computer-Mediated Communication*, 3(2).

Low, S., and Altman, I. (1992). Place attachment: A conceptual inquiry. In Altman, I., and Low, S. (Eds.), *Place Attachment* (pp. 1–13). New York, NY: Plenum Press. doi:10.1525/sp.1967.15.2.03a00090

Lyman, S., and Scott, M. (1967). Territoriality: A neglected sociological dimension. *Social Problems*, 15(2), pp. 236–249.

Lynch, K. (1960). *The Image of the City*. Cambridge, MA: MIT Press. doi:10.1145/1067860.1067864

Maloney-Krichmar, D., and Preece, J. (2005). A multilevel analysis of sociability, usability and community dynamics in an online health community. *Transactions on Human-Computer Interaction*, 12(2), pp. 201–232.

Marmasse, N., and Schmandt, C. (2000). Location-aware information delivery with ComMotion. In *Proceedings of HUC'00*, pp. 157–171, Bristol, UK. doi:10.1002/aris.1440370107

Marty, P., Rayward, W., and Twidale, M. (2003). Museum informatics. In Cronin, B. (Ed.), *Annual Review of Information Science and Technology*, 37 (pp. 259–294). Medford, MA: Information Today.

Massey, D. (1997). A global sense of place. In: Cresswell, T. (2004) (Ed.), *Place: A Short Introduction* (pp. 63–70). Malden, MA: Blackwell.

McKenna, K., Postmes, T., and Reips, U. (Eds.) (2007). *The Oxford handbook of Internet psychology*. Oxford, UK: University Press.

Messaris, P. (1997). *Visual Persuasion: The Role of Images in Advertising*. Thousand Oaks, CA: Sage.

McCarthy, J., and Wright, P. (2003). Making sense of experience. In Blythe, M., Monk, A., Overbeeke, C., and Wright, P. (Eds.), *Funology: From Usability to User Enjoyment*. Dordrecht, Netherlands: Kluwer.

Munro, A., Höök, K., and Benyon, D. (1999). *Social Navigation of Information Space*. Berlin: Springer-Verlag.

Nardi, B. (1996). *Context and Consciousness: Activity Theory and Human–Computer Interaction*, pp. 1–20. Cambridge, MA: MIT Press.

Nardi, B., and Whittaker, S. (2002). The place of face-to-face communication in distributed work. In Hinds, P., and Kiesler, S. (Eds.), *Distributed Work* (pp. 83–113). Boston, MA: MIT Press.

Norman, D. (1988). *The Psychology of Everyday Things*. New York, NY: Basic Books. doi:10.1145/192844.192871

Okamura, K. (1994). Helping CSCW applications succeed: The role of mediators in the context of use. In *Proceedings of CSCW'94*, Chapel Hill, NC.

O'Keefe, D. (2002). *Persuasion, Theory and Research*. Thousand Oaks, CA: Sage.

Olson, G., and Olson, J. (2001). Distance matters. *Human-Computer Interaction*, 15, pp. 139–179.

Ortony, A., Clore, G., and Collins, A. (1988). *The Cognitive Structure of Emotions*. New York, NY: Cambridge Press. doi:10.1145/238218.238344

Pascoe, J. (1997). The Stick-e note architecture: Extending the interface beyond the user. In *Proceedings of ICIUI'97*, pp. 261–264, Edinburgh, Scotland.

Picard, R. (1997). *Affective Computing*. Cambridge, MA: MIT Press. doi:10.1016/S0953-5438(98)00056-3

Preece, J. (1999a). Empathic communities: Balancing emotional and factual communication. *Interacting with Computers*, 12(1), pp. 63–77. doi:10.1007/BF01434996

Preece, J. (1999b). Empathy online. *Virtual Reality*, 4(1), pp. 74–84. doi:10.1145/215585.215639

Rekimoto, J., and Nagao, K. (1995). The world through the computer: Computer augmented interaction with real world environments. In *Proceedings of ACM'95*, pp. 29–38, Pittsburgh, PA.

Rogers, E. (2003). *Diffusion of Innovation (5th edition)*. New York, NY: Free Press.

Schachter, S. (1959). *The Psychology of Affiliation*. Stanford, CA: Stanford University Press. doi:10.1037/h0046234

Schachter, S., and Singer, J. (1962). Cognitive, social and physiological determinants of emotional state. *Psychological Review*, 69, pp. 379–399.

Seamon, D. (1979). *A Geography of Lifeworld: Movement, Rest and Encounter*. London, UK: Croom Helm.

Sengers, P. (2004). The agents of McDonaldization. In: Payr, S., and Trappl, R. (Eds.), *Agent culture: Human–agent interaction in a multicultural world*, pp. 3–20, Hillsdale, NJ: Erlbaum. doi:10.1007/s00779-007-0161-4

Sengers, P., Boehner, K., Mateas, M., and Gay, G. (2008). The disenchantment of affect. *Journal of Pervasive and Ubiquitous Computing*, 12(5), pp. 347–358.

Shannon, C. (1948). A mathematical theory of communication. *Bell System Technical Journal*, 27, pp. 379–656.

Short, J., Williams, E., and Christie, B. (1976). *The Social Psychology of Telecommunications*. London, UK: Wiley.

Sparacino, F. (2002). The museum wearable. In *Proceedings of Museums and the Web'02*. Electronic proceedings http://www.archimuse.com/mw2002/abstracts/prg_165000836.html. doi:10 .1145/173668.168641

Spreitzer, M., and Theimer, M. (1993). Providing location information in a ubiquitous computing environment. In *Proceedings of AMC'93*, pp. 270–283, Asheville, NC. doi:10.1146/annurev .soc.24.1.265

Strang, D., and Soule, S. (1998). Diffusion in organizations and social movements: From hybrid corn to poison pills. *Annual Review of Sociology*, 24, pp. 265–290. doi:10.1007/s11257-007-9029-6

Stock, O., Zancanaro, M., Busetta, P., Callaway, C., Krüger, A., Kruppa, M., Kuflik, T., Not, E., and Rocchi, C. (2007). Intelligent presentation of information for the museum visitor in PEACH. *User-Modeling and User-Adapted Interaction*, 17(3), pp. 257–304.

Suchman, L. (1987). *Plans and Situated Actions*. Cambridge, UK: Cambridge University Press. doi:10.1111/1467-8721.00191

Suls, J., Martin, R., and Wheeler, L. (2002). Social comparison: Why, with whom and with what effect? *Current Directions in Psychological Science*, 11(5), pp. 159–163. doi:10.1016/ j.ijhcs.2006.11.013

Sundström, P., Ståhl, A., and Höök, K. (2007). In-situ informants exploring an emotional mobile messaging system in their everyday practice. *International Journal of Human-Computer Studies*, 65(4), pp. 388–403.

Thom-Santelli, J., Toma, C., Boehner, K., and Gay, G. (2005). Beyond just the facts: Museum detective guides. Re-Thinking Technology in Museums Workshop, Limerick, Ireland.

Trant, J., Bearman D., and Chun, S. (2007). The eye of the beholder: Steve.museum and social tagging of museum collections. In *Proceedings of ICHIM'07*, Toronto, Canada. doi:10.1145/ 1357054.1357133

Troshynski, E., Lee, C., and Dourish, P. (2008). Accountabilities of presence: Reframing location-based systems. In *Proceedings of CHI'08*, pp. 487–496, Florence, Italy.

Trumbull, D., Gay, G., and Mazur J. (1992). Students' actual and perceived use of navigational and guidance tools in a hypermedia program, *Journal of Research on Computing in Education*, 4(3), pp. 315–329.

Truax, B. (2001). *Acoustic Communication*. Westport, CT: Ablex.

Tuan, Y. F. (1977). *Space and Place: The Perspective of Experience*. Minneapolis, MN: University of Minnesota Press. doi:10.1016/0378-8733(95)00256-1

Valente, T. W. (1996). Social network thresholds in the diffusion of innovations. *Social Networks*, 18(1), pp. 69–89. doi:10.1145/302979.302981

Viegas, F., and Donath, J. (1999). Chat circles. In *Proceedings of CHI'99*, pp. 9–16, Pittsburgh, PA.

Wallace, P. (1999). *Psychology of the Internet*. New York, NY: Cambridge University Press. doi:10.1111/j.1460-2466.2005.tb02688.x

Walther, J., Gay, G., and Hancock, J. (2005). How do communication and technology researchers study the Internet? *Journal of Communication*, 55, pp. 632–657.

Wansink, B. (2006). *Mindless Eating: Why We Eat More Than We Think*. New York, NY: Bantam Dell. doi:10.2307/3151931

Wansink, B., Kent, R., and Hoch S. (1998). An anchoring and adjustment model of purchase quantity decisions. *Journal of Marketing Research*, 35, pp. 71–81. doi:10.1145/128756.128759

Want, R., Hooper, A., Falcao, V., and Gibbons, J. (1992). The active badge location system. *ACM Transactions on Information Systems*, 10(1), pp. 91–102.

Wenger, E. (1998). *Communities of Practice: Learning, Meaning, and Identity*. New York, NY: Cambridge University Press.

Whyte, W. (1988). *City: Rediscovering the Center*. New York, NY: Doubleday. doi:10.1207/S15327051HCI16234_18

Winograd, T. (2001): Architectures for context. *Human-Computer Interaction*, 16(2), pp. 401–419.

Wood, W. (2003). Attitude change: Persuasion and social influence. *Annual Review of Psychology*, 51, pp. 539–570.

Woodruff, A., Aoki, P., Hurst, A., and Szymanski, M. H. (2001). Electronic guidebooks and visitor attention. In *Proceedings of ICHIM'01*, Milan, Italy. doi:10.1111/j.1083-6101.2006.00308.x

Yuan, Y., and Gay, G. (2006). Homophily of network ties, and bonding and bridging social capital in distributed teams. *Journal of Computer-Mediated Communication*, 11(4). doi:10.1126/science.149.3681.269

Zajonc, R. (1965). Social facilitation. *Science*, 149, pp. 269–274.

Author Biography

Geri Gay is the Kenneth J. Bissett Professor and Chair of Communication at Cornell University and a Stephen H. Weiss Presidential Fellow. She is also a member of the Faculty of Computer and Information Science and the director of the Human Computer Interaction Laboratory at Cornell University. Her research focuses on social and technical issues in the design of interactive communication technologies. Specifically, she is interested in social navigation, affective computing, social networking, mobile computing, and design theory.

Prof. Gay has received funding for her research and design projects from NSF, NASA, the Mellon Foundation, Intel, Google, Microsoft, NIH, the Robert Wood Johnson Foundation, AT&T Foundation, and several private donors. She teaches courses in interactive multimedia design and research, computer-mediated communication, human–computer interaction, and the social design of communication systems.

Recently, she has published in *IEEE, International Journal of Human-Computer Interaction, Journal of Computer-Mediated Communication, Journal of Communication, CHI, HICCS, ACM Digital Libraries, SIGIR, JASIST*, and *CSCW*.

Printed in the United States
by Baker & Taylor Publisher Services